HOW TO SELL YOUR HIGHER PRICE

Also by the same author:

Close Close Close
How to Win New Customers
Selling – the Most Important Job in the World
101 Ways to Boost Your Performance
How to Double Your Profits Within the Year
How to Get the Best Out of Today's Salespeople

HOW TO SELL YOUR HIGHER PRICE

John Fenton

2000

First published in 1998 by Management Books 2000 Ltd

This revised edition published in 2002 by Management Books 2000 Ltd
Forge House, Limes Road
Kemble, Cirencester
Gloucestershire GL7 6AD
tel: 01285 771441/2   fax: 01285 771055
E-mail: mb2000@compuserve.com

Printed and bound in Great Britain by Biddles, Guildford

British Library Cataloguing in Publication Data is available
ISBN 1-85252-411-1

Contents

JOHN FENTON doesn't just write books. He is in great demand as a **MAKING IT HAPPEN** management consultant and trainer, as the testimonials on these two pages demonstrate:

"I was surprised what opportunities we as a Company were missing."
Timothy Jackson
Somers Handling Limited

"It really worked. This has been the best selling year in our history. New orders are more than 40% up on last year and success stories spread across every product line and every sales area."
Philip Bullus
Bournes Electronics Limited

"We have actually managed to increase our business over the past two years by 25% per year, a lot of which could not have been achieved had we not used the information and ideas given by you."
Dick Goodall
Aquatech Marketing Limited

"It gave us the answers to questions we didn't even know we should be asking - AND practical solutions to many other problems."
Richard Frost
Barpro Storage Systems

"Excellent, stimulating, practical, true, feasible, vital."
A. E. Judd
Industrial Division - Crane Heatex

"Mind Blowing."
Phil Cooper
Abbotts Packaging Limited

"Impressive and important. Can't fail to improve results."
Peter McArthur
Link 51

"Really worthwhile and absolutely worth every penny."
Vincent Brinkhof
Standard & Poor's

"So many simple ideas that can greatly increase our business."
Angus Beston
Protim Solignum Ltd

"Excellent. It has provided many new ideas."
Roger Chadwick
Labeltech Ltd

"Many managerial tips for steering our 'ship' through the stormy waters of this unending recession."
Brett Hacket
William Hacket Ltd

"Excellent. A great deal of food for thought, plus months of Action Plans."
David Broadbent
Northern Joinery Ltd

"VERY good. Refreshed old ideas and gave a valued injection of Fentonisms. All parts were relevant."
Alan Pearson
Thermon (UK) Ltd

"Excellent. It generated precise logical thinking in preparing a structured plan to increase business."
Mike Turness
Thomas Sanderson Blinds Ltd

"Thank you for an enlightening day of Action Planning."
Richard Leonard
British Industrial Sand Ltd

"I've come back brimming full of new plans for increasing sales - and re-charged personally."
Peter Yeats
Lilleshall Steels Ltd

To discuss what **JOHN FENTON** can do for your business, write, fax tel. or e-mail to **John Fenton Stratagems Plc.**

Clifford Hill Court, Clifford Chambers, Stratford upon Avon, CV37 8AA
Tel: 01789 266716 or 298739 Fax: 01789 266409 or 294442 E-mail: fenton@waverider.co.uk

"If you want to turn quotes into orders, you need to make these changes."
Magda Sargent
Guardsman Limited

"Identified shortcomings of existing quotation format. New and different approaches to increase conversion rate. Objectives fully achieved."
Graham McKenzie
Riverside Plastics Limited

"Thank you. Quoting has stopped my business committing commercial suicide."
Stuart Gizzi
Altecnic Limited

"Excellent. It made me step into my customer shoes."
Alan Squires
Flexiprint Limited

"Many new ideas on how to make the customer more aware and how to incorporate more of the essential information that we tend to take for granted."
Andy Hunt
Anti-static Technology Limited

"It made my thought process open out, especially on how to support a formal tender with valid and valuable material and improve the presentation."
Brian Burchell
Robinson Healthcare

"I learnt how to modularly produce quotations to suit my customers' needs instead of my own. It has inspired me to change possibly ALL aspects of how we quote."
Charlotte Foster
Computionics Limited

"Brought out many errors in current practice and will enable us to move from legal quotations to selling proposals."
A. E. Poeton
A T Poeton & Son Limited

"Our retained margin has in creased by 8%, our proposals to order ratio has halved, from 8 to 1 down to 4 to 1 and the number of testimonials increases daily."
Steve Wall
Gearhouse Ltd

"Your input on how we quote meant that we improved turnover by 20% on last year and maintained our margin."
Eddie Mander
CGS Catering Equipment

"Your CFO List has given us an edge not one of our 400 competitors can beat."
Ian Garner
The Hobart Manufacturing Co. Ltd

"Your proposal folder, testimonials and CFO List will give us another £10 million sales over the next three years, for the same number of quotations."
Chris Smith
Southern Print (Web Offset) Ltd

"So far, I've had 100% success closing proposals that I've produced since you gave us the know-how."
Martin Sewell
Marketing Initiatives Ltd

"Our Quotes to Order Ratio has improved from 25 to 1 down to 4.5 to 1 since you gave us the treatment. That's 5.5 times as many Orders from the same number of Quotations."
Ernie Johnson
GKN Sankey Limited

VISION STATEMENT

The Profession of Selling

It is a glaring glimpse of the obvious to say that no amount of production is the slightest value unless the products are sold for cash.

Selling is the very crux of any commercial or industrial enterprise.

It therefore stands to reason that, as a nation which depends so heavily on selling our products abroad, it is very much in the national interest that the highest standards and the most advanced techniques in salesmanship should be encouraged.

HRH Prince Philip

Duke of Edinburgh KG, KT

Foreword

Don't believe the Media

What credibility has the Media – newspapers, radio, television – which crucifies Selling at every opportunity, yet still refers to it often as "The Second Oldest Profession"?

Note the word PROFESSION.

Okay, just like any other profession, including solicitors, accountants and bankers, there are and always will be those few bad eggs which the Media will be quick to headline. But notwithstanding this, let us not have any argument about it – Selling should be TOP of the league table of professions.

It IS top in America. Why it isn't in Great Britain and many other countries is more down to the Media than to all other reasons put together. And the Media has brainwashed the education established to the extent that our schools actively discourage pupils away from any serious thought of a career in Selling.

In the Vision Statement to this book, HRH Prince Philip, the Duke of Edinburgh says:

"Selling is the very crux of any commercial or industrial enterprise."

Positive, dynamic, enthusiastic Selling can do more to boost the economy and increase employment than anything else. And do it faster than anything else. In all walks of life, Selling is as essential as food and drink.

Customers don't beat a path to many doors these days. Only when someone develops something extraordinarily better or half the price of what went before. Everywhere else the inertia of human nature (bone idleness) causes the minimum to be purchased – unless sales promotion stimulates interest and salespeople convert that interest into orders.

In industry, if the salespeople at the 'sharp end' didn't sell, just about everybody in manufacturing and distributing would be out of a job. Same for the service industries.

In retail stores and at trade exhibitions, if customers were just left to browse and salespeople didn't try to positively create a specific interest and help those browsers decide to buy, very little actual business would happen.

Author's Health Warning

SELLING IS THE MOST EXCITING

THING YOU CAN DO

WITH YOUR CLOTHES ON

We're never going to be the biggest,
so we're going to be the best'

Chapter 1

How to Sell Quality

Once upon a time there was a Seller's Market

Customers clamoured to buy. Supply could not satisfy demand. Manufacturers swiftly developed new techniques of mass production, mechanisation, and automation, to try to cope with the demand for hitherto hand-made products. Craftsmanship was sacrificed at the altar of volume.

It was called The Industrial Revolution.

It began 150 years ago. It was held back a few times by economic catastrophes like The Great Depression. It was stimulated by a few wars. It finally died in the mid-1970s when the Middle East marmalized Western Civilization by wopping up the price of oil.

Since then, we have been witnessing a fundamental change in people's buying habits. No longer do people buy what they can get. No longer do they buy just on price – the cheapest price they can find. (And if you don't believe this, just ask a few people what car they drive, and see how many have bought the lowest-priced car that would do the job they needed it to do).

We have entered the *second* Industrial Revolution.

The first was based on *quantity*. The second Industrial Revolution is based on *quality*. That's what people will be buying from now on. I don't think the Seller's Market will be back in our lifetime. We've grown too intelligent!

Selling the Best is the Easiest

In Selling, the maximum job satisfaction, the maximum fun and the maximum rewards come from selling the best product or service at the *highest* price. It is also *easiest* when selling at this level, if the selling is done properly and if you are aiming for maximum profit, not maximum volume. In other words, you don't want to be the biggest supplier in your particular market, just the best.

No one will ever convince me that this is not so, because I've personally tested the theory and proved it fact, time and time again.

Okay, only one supplier in any market can hold the Quality number one spot. The rest have to make do with second, third, fourth best, down to worst. The higher you can get in the Quality league table, however, the better – and climbing up this league table is much easier and much less expensive than most businesses think.

There is no substitute for a really good product or a really good service, of course, but at the same time there is no point in making the product or service too good, if the market does not require anything better than is currently available. Thus, several suppliers can climb the Quality league table and, on product or service, performance, reliability and all the other 'tangibles', find themselves all at exactly the same level, if their market dictates terms in this way.

If this is your problem, a more intangible form of quality comes into play, known as **Perceived Value.**

Perceived Value

Roughly translated, Perceived Value means if the product or service and its trappings *look, feel, smell or taste* more expensive than those of other suppliers, then the customers are likely to be happy to pay slightly more for them, or be less demanding on discounts!

By 'trappings', I mean everything that goes to make up the supplier's Corporate Image. Consider the 'trappings' shown as pieces of a jigsaw puzzle. Each piece is an essential part of the complete picture – the Corporate Image. If one or two pieces don't fit, then the complete picture falls asunder. So it is with a supplier's Corporate Image. All the pieces must be made to fit the picture that you want to portray to your customers. **ALL THE PIECES** – because you do not know which piece or pieces a customer will be looking at at a particular point in time. Few customers will see ALL of them at the same time, and the pieces that are seen, to the customer will be the WHOLE picture.

It's a question of Aesthetics. The overall impression of you and your company – as a better supplier – that is seen by the customer; that is *perceived* by the customer. The dictionary definition of the word Aesthetics is 'the perception of the beautiful'. As long as you don't put it in the context of conning people, the old saying 'What you believe is more important than the truth' might fit the bill.

Everyone in the world is looking for something better at no extra cost. Maybe you are seeking, as a business, to *maintain* your prices while your competitors are cutting theirs. To do this, you have to sell the intangible form of Quality. You have to make the customers *believe* they are getting something better – getting more for their money if they buy from you.

In periods of stiff recession, Selling Quality can be the key to survival while the competitors go down the tubes.

Let's examine what might be done to improve the pieces of this particular Corporate Image jigsaw puzzle.

 Let's start by looking in the hall mirror, first thing in the morning, just about to leave home for a hard day in the field. There you are, newly pressed suit, clean silk handkerchief in top pocket, subdued tie, polished shoes, smart briefcase, hair brushed and recently trimmed, teeth brushed, no blood clots from shaving, faint smell of Eau Sauvage in the air. Not a bad sight for so early in the morning. But wait! Put yourself in the customer's shoes.

Would *you* buy *anything* better from a guy like *you*?

Look in that mirror and think about it. How different do YOU look from that 'not bad' early morning sight two paragraphs back? That briefcase is a family heirloom and hasn't seen a tin of polish in 20 years. That bright red tie isn't really what you'd call subdued, is it? And those three pens clipped in your top pocket – they give you an identity more like a clerk than an executive. The mud on your shoes and trouser turn-ups doesn't show much, but what about when you sit down next to the customer in half an hour's time. Knees a bit baggy, but the suit'll do for another week before it's due for the dry cleaners. Been meaning to get to the hairdressers for about three months now, but there's always been too many people waiting. Maybe next week.

Do I need to say any more? If you cannot get this bit right – *every single selling day* – then there's not much hope for either you or your Corporate Image.

If you yourself *look* more expensive, you'll get less hassle and price objections from your customers and a hell of a lot more respect from everyone – receptionist up to managing director. But don't overdo it. Just look the part.

Talking about respect, there's another kind of respect important in the Corporate Image jigsaw puzzle - the respect you give your company and your products.

Salespeople at the top of the Quality league table never ever moan about their company, or any of its personnel, or its products. They never run anything down. They never pass the buck. If a mistake is made, *they* carry the can and take the blame, even if it was someone else's mistake. They praise their company, its personnel, and its products, at every opportunity. They show pride in everything they do. And the customer gets the message.

Salespeople at the top of the Quality league table never abuse or denigrate their products or services by their actions. They never kick or slap or toss them around. They treat their products with the utmost respect and, as a result, their products come over as superior in the eyes of their customers.

If you're selling the best pocket calculator on the market, it's no good tossing it to a customer and saying: 'What do you think of that?' Hand it to him reverently and say: 'I'd like your opinion of our new calculator. We think it's the very best that's been produced so far'.

There's a true story about two company directors who set out one day to look for a quantity of five drawer filing cabinets. They wanted to see the cabinets for themselves before ordering.

They called at one large office equipment supplier. 'Yes', said the salesman, 'we've got some very good five drawer filing cabinets. Here is one, over here.'

The salesman proceeded to show off the filing cabinet to the two directors. 'Very strong, these are', he extolled, slapping the side of the cabinet – doiiinnggg! Empty cabinets make a lot of tinny noise! 'Drawers have very smooth action, rollers all the way, good strong stops to prevent the drawers falling out.' The salesman flicked open a drawer so that it shot out to its full reach and jarred against its stops. Then he flicked it back in again and the drawer bounced out from its shut position. With a nudge of his elbow, the salesman pushed the drawer properly shut. Prices and delivery were discussed and the two directors departed with the promise that they would give the purchase serious consideration. The filing cabinet they'd seen would certainly do the job they wanted done.

They found another large office equipment supplier. 'Yes', said the salesman, a more refined type and some 15 years older, 'we do indeed have some very good quality five drawer filing cabinets. Would you care to follow me?'

The salesman introduced the two directors to his filing cabinet. He didn't slap it; he flicked a speck of dust off its top. When he opened and closed the drawer, he kept his hand on the drawer handle all the time, so that the drawer slid open and shut without a sound other than the smooth rumble of the rollers in their tracks. The cabinet was a different colour from the first one they'd seen, but perfectly acceptable.

Price and delivery were discussed. The cabinets were £25 each more expensive than the first ones they'd examined. The two directors departed to continue their search, but by the end of the day they hadn't found any more suppliers with five drawer filing cabinets. They discussed the pros and cons of the two cabinets they'd seen and agreed that the second cabinet was of much better quality than the first. They ordered the better quality cabinets, notwithstanding the £25 extra price.

The point of this story is that both cabinets were manufactured on the same production line at the same time. Only the colour and labelling was different, to the specification of each office equipment supplier. But no one would have convinced those two directors that this was so.

That's the intangible part of Selling Quality.

You won't believe the incredible blunders companies make on colours; blunders made in all innocence, because the powers-that-be know nothing about the Corporate Image jigsaw puzzle. If I may quote a far greater guru than me: 'God forgive them for they know not what they do.'

There was a classic example at the International Machine Tool Exhibition. One exhibitor was introducing two new machines into its existing range of machines. The whole range, including the two new models, ran in a line across the front of the exhibition stand. The two new machines were better, faster, more reliable, produced better quality components and, of course, were more expensive.

But very few visitors to the exhibition showed interest in buying the new models. All the interest was on the existing range. The powers-that-be couldn't understand it, yet the reason stuck out like a sore thumb.

The colour scheme for the existing range of machines was a nice, darker shade of British Racing Green with the guards over the moving parts finished in a subdued yellow. The combination was very pleasing to the eye. The two new models, however, were painted in a different colour. The powers-that-be had decided, before the exhibition, that the new models should be painted a different colour for the show so that they stood out on the stand. An instruction was passed to the paint shop. 'Paint new models in a different colour'. No thought was given to what colour, or why. The paint shop used what paints they had in stock and mixed a special. They knew nothing about the Corporate Image jigsaw puzzle either.

The resulting colour scheme for the new models was a particularly bilious shade of what I call 'Puke Green' with the guards in bright orange. To the eye of the beholder, the beauty had been turned into 'Cheap and Cheerful'.

For the exhibitor to convince its customers that the two new models were better than the existing range was henceforth next to impossible. They didn't look better, they looked inferior,

It's that easy to get it wrong. Why has Lansing Bagnall, one of the UK's largest fork lift truck manufacturers, always finished its trucks in a rich dark red, while all the other manufacturers have finished theirs in yellow? Because the rich dark red bestows an aura of quality on the LB trucks that none of the yellow trucks can match.

The Alfred Herbert group, long before its demise, was reputed to have spent a lot of money having a new Corporate Identity prepared for it. The main theme of the new CI was a colour – a special magenta. But it was a down-market colour and *reduced* the perceived value of the company in the eyes of its customers. It was also hellish difficult to re-produce, which probably added 20% to Herbert's print bills. This major blunder must have cost the company millions in lost business and speeded up a death which otherwise might have been avoided.

The natural colours project quality best - the buffs, the beiges, the creams, the mushrooms, the creamy browns, the leaf and olive greens. Yellows, oranges and bright greens are cheap and cheerful. Reds can be cheap, if post-office red, or expensive if Mercedes red. Blues can be good or bad with subtle differences in shade taking a product ten points up or down the league table. Combinations can do more for quality than single colours. A two-tone cabinet in light grey and dark grey comes over very well. Black and green gives a good result. Black and satin aluminium, or black and gold, is superb – think about the effect John Player Special and Benson & Hedges get from their cigarette packets. Yellow and red is a dangerous combination. Yet Kodak has made it work wonderfully well. It depends on the product.

The colour of a salesperson's suit, tie, shirt, socks, briefcase and company car all contribute to the Corporate Image picture which the customer sees. All should be carefully and consciously assessed and efforts made to increase their quality factors.

UK publishers Mitchell Beazley Ltd brought out a book on the subject, entitled *Colour* which presented the many complexities of using colour in business in an easy-to-understand and very comprehensive form. Here is a short quote from this extremely valuable book:

'The language of colour is a vital living thing, our most potent means of perception and communication. It impinges on our every waking moment and even invades our sleep. Consciously or subconsciously, it influences every decision we make.

Today's supermarkets present an avalanche of coloured tins, packets, jars and bottles, all carefully calculated to catch our attention and convince us to buy. Some succeed – J-Cloths, for example, are reputed to have boosted sales some 23% by an apparently simple change in coloured packaging – others fail and vanish forever... why?

And why is it that the safest, most sensible colours for cars – the ones which show up best in poor light – are the ones we are least likely to choose?

Even the clothes we wear pose some intriguing questions about our reactions to colour – why blue jeans, for example, and not brown or red or green?

Colours are the basic elements of the modern alchemist's art – "the magic touch that can turn dross into gold". Red is warm. Blue is cool. Yellow is cheerful. Black depresses ... sometimes. But the human eye can distinguish some ten million variations in colour, so we mix them together and seek to "cast a spell".

Colour can dictate our moods and condition our reflexes. It has been used successfully in factories to increase production, cut absenteeism and prevent accidents – and in boardrooms to reduce aggression and enhance decision-making.

Today, in our modern, sophisticated and often artificial world, our skilful use of colour becomes ever more important – we must even colour much of the food we eat to make it acceptable. 'Yet, not surprisingly, few of us can claim any real fluency in this most potent of all languages.'

 Consider the two advertisements on the next page. They are both mono (black and white). They are both half a page vertical in an A4-size trade magazine. How does the Corporate Image of the company advertising come over to you?

Which is the quality company? Which is the cheap and cheerful company? It's obvious, isn't it? But only the choice of words, pictures and type style is different

On type styles, serif faces tend to project better quality than sans faces (serif has the twiddly bits, like Times Roman; sans is just plain, like Univers. Get a book of type faces free from your printers to see what options are available to you.)

Advertisements don't have to be full colour and big to project quality. Small classified adverts can do it just as well, providing the type style is right and there's plenty of white space. Obviously, a full page in full colour gives more scope, but many a business has let its advertising agency mess it all up by allowing the agency to pursue a gimmick idea in bold lurid colours. Sometimes it bashes a dirty great hole in the Corporate Image that takes months to patch up.

Again, the natural colours are best in advertisements that aim to upgrade Quality. Use photographs with real people in them – people who look as good as your Salespeople should look. Above all, don't ever use heavily touched up 'still-life' pictures of the products.

The same thing applies to your other kinds of sales promotion, mail-shots, press releases, exhibition stands and business gifts.

Let's dwell for a couple of minutes on business gifts. These are not just restricted to Christmas time, although calendars and diaries, of course, always will be. Don't get business gifts that are part of sales promotion mixed up with gifts that are 'Thank You's' for past business, such as bottles of whisky and a dinner for four at a sumptuous restaurant or club.

A business gift promotes business. It should be designed for use or display by your customers and prospective customers in or at their place of business, Okay, if you do business in their homes, that's the place.

Business gifts should have the longest possible life and should always carry your business name, address and telephone number – in the right place! (I've seen cubic memo pads with the supplier's number printed on all four sides, *at the top*! So after the first 50 or so sheets of the pads have been used by the customers, the gift becomes useless – the telephone number has gone!)

Business gifts should always reflect your Corporate Image. If you're seeking to go up-market in the Quality league table, it's no good spreading around a cheap and cheerful business gift. Likewise, if you're at the bottom of the league table and happy to stay there, you'd be wasting your money on quality business gifts.

The very best business gifts are tailor-made for specific, very good customers. They give the customer much pleasure, they demoralise your competitors' salespeople and they really stimulate your salesforce. Here's one of my favourites:

Let's assume you have a budget for this particular very good customer that would buy you a case of good whisky. But the last thing you want to do is spend the money on whisky. Once drunk, soon forgotten, and usually taken home. You know a lot about this customer. You know his hobbies and his habits, his likes and his dislikes. You know he's a sailing fanatic – every weekend, out on the reservoir. Small dinghy, but dreams about something much better and much bigger.

You're sitting in his office. You've concluded business. You have your eye on a particular section of his office wall, above his bookcase. You dangle the carrot.

'I've been wondering about that piece of wall above your bookcase, Mr Arnold.' He looks somewhat puzzled. You go on. 'My company has been putting together some rather different sales promotion gifts for this year; a bit out of the ordinary you might say. Just for our very best customers. One of the ideas we've come up with is to produce some original oil paintings, each one on a particular subject.

'One of the artists we've commissioned is pretty near as good as Montague Dawson. His seascapes are fantastic. I was thinking how nice a painting of that 46 footer you told me about last time I was here, would look over your bookcase, with Cowes or something similar in the background.'

You watch his eyes light up. His posture changes from casually relaxed to keenly interested. 'What sort of frame do you think would be most suitable?' you ask.

Just 10 minutes later, you have the full specification for the picture and the frame, plus a brochure containing a colour picture of the 46 footer he's always wanted but will never be able to afford.

Your sales promotion people make contact with a few young artists. (If you're in London on a Sunday, just walk down Piccadilly and see how many you can find who will do you a *good* original oil for under £50, In Worcester there are 40 young artists who have joined together as a syndicate to produce and sell paintings. Good artists are falling off trees!)

Two months later, you deliver the finished, framed, oil painting. Inset into the lower horizontal frame is an engraved brass plate, which reads:

Presented to Walter Arnold
by Acme Distributions Limited
November 1997

You've come armed with picture hooks, hammer, measuring tape, and pliers (just in case!). You and he spend a happy half-hour hanging the picture over the bookcase. Then you both sit back for a few minutes, drinking coffee and admiring the picture before you get down to the business reason for this particular visit.

Your picture is there for life – or for the life of Walter Arnold as an

26

executive of that company. He can't take the picture home without offending you and your company greatly. It serves as a constant reminder of what a professional, top quality supplier is really like. And every time one of your competitors sits in that office, he's grinding his teeth, dying to say to Mr Arnold, 'Why do you keep that dreadful picture hanging there? We could give you something much better than that'.

But the competitors know they can never say that. That's demoralisation for you!

The Pirelli Calendar Classic

Throughout the 1960s, one particular business gift became a legend in its own lifetime – the Pirelli Calendar.

By 1970, if you wanted one, it was a question of how many tyres you ordered, rather than how much you'd pay for the calendar. By 1980, you could get £100 for an *old* Pirelli calendar.

As perhaps you'd expect, one of my companies consults on rather different business gifts. I've been working on one in particular which I reckon could be as good as the Pirelli Calendar. It lends itself to a large organisation that has divisions in each region of the UK. Let's assume there are seven divisions.

My business gift is a set of seven limited edition prints, all nicely framed. The subject matter for the prints is classified (sorry) but of universal appeal and a certain laughter generator. Each of the seven divisions uses *only one* of the set of prints in any one year, but each division uses a *different* one of the set. Thus, the business gift has a full seven years life and 'collectors' of the limited edition set have to stay doing business with a division for that long to be sure of securing the complete set. The organisation's name, address and telephone number, and the name of the customer who receives the print, are included in a particularly ingenious way.

Of course, you *can* secure the complete set in the first year, but, like Pirelli, that depends on how much of the product you buy!

Calendars – the normal kind, girlie or whatever – are not very good business gifts, because, like diaries, they depend upon the personal choice of the customer. The customer probably receives a dozen calendars and a dozen diaries from his suppliers every Christmas. What is going to make him select and display only yours?

If you buy 1,000 similar calendars or diaries, you'll be lucky if 100 are ever used by the people to whom you give them. Consider your own diary. How long have you used that particular format? Will you want to continue using that same format next year, because you're used to it? Chances are you will. So if you are given a diary of a different format, you'll probably pass it on to someone else. You'll even go out and *buy* the diary you really like using, if you have to. Customers are no different.

Calendars also have a very short life. One year maximum. Your business gifts should last longer that that. The best calendar I've ever developed so that it is nearly always selected by the customers for display in their offices and has an unlimited life is, in fact, useless as a calendar. This is the now famous Rush Jobs Calendar. Here is the version used by my own organisation, where every day is a potential Mirday. Every day in your business could be, too!

Rush Job Calendar

Mir	Fri	Fri	Fri	Thu	Wed	Tue
8	7	6	5	4	3	2
15	14		12	11	10	9
22	21	20	19	18	17	16
29	28	27	26	25	24	23
36	35	34	33	32	31	30

This is a special calendar which has been developed to handle 'rush jobs'. As all rush jobs are wanted yesterday, dates run backwards so that work ordered on the 7th can be delivered on the 3rd. The 13th is omitted to please the superstitious. There are three Fridays in every week because everybody wants his job done by Friday. Five new days at the end of the month cater for 'end-of-month' jobs, late completion of which is discouraged by having no 1st of the month. Mondays have been abolished because nobody likes them. There are no Saturdays or Sundays so that overtime payments can be kept to a minimum. Every week includes a special day – MIRDAY – for the performance of miracles.

If you want to rise to near the top of your market's Quality league table, then the letters you write and the letterheads you write them on must be top notch. You need the latest word-processors. Layout of the letters carefully thought out. Wide margins. Lots of space. Short, easily read paragraphs. Meaningful, quality-oriented words.

I spend a fair bit of my time copy-writing. Often I'm asked to advise on why a certain standard sales letter or circular isn't achieving the required results. Here is an example, together with my suggested improved letter. Hopefully, this will guide you into writing your own better letters that will bring this piece in the jigsaw puzzle up to its desired position.

Letter

The company in question is already in the top three in its market's Quality league table.

Re: Pre-qualification – Commercial Catering Equipment

We would confirm our interest in pre-qualifying for the supply and installation of Commercial Catering Equipment for your various projects.

As part of ... we have first-hand experience in all types of catering operations while our corporate buying power renders us truly competitive. Whatever your requirement, we can offer a partial or total service covering all aspects from free planning and design, to supply, installation, commissioning and, if required, even maintenance. Where needed we can also offer an integrated package including building works and services installation, restaurant furnishing and equipment.

As requested, we enclose herewith a copy of our brochure, which outlines our organisation and its capabilities and would welcome the opportunity of providing any additional information you may require.

Yours faithfully

Full of Victoriana, stilted phrases, strange terminology (pre-qualifying means 'can we go on your list of approved suppliers?') and rather cheaply duplicated so that it was impossible to match in the recipient's address without shouting to him that it is a circular, not a personal, letter.

Writing better letters isn't *just* for the Corporate Image jigsaw piece. Any selling letter must live and breathe; be full of carrots and benefits; tell the prospective customer what's in it for him, not just what you, the writer, have done; although the letter must finish with what you are *after* – what you want the prospective customer to do or what *you* intend to do.

There is a clear-cut formula for selling letters – AIDA. In strict order, start to finish: Attention, Interest, Desire, Action. Follow this formula, make your letter live, use words which bestow status, rather than give a cheap and cheerful impression, use the best quality paper and laser printer, and you won't go far wrong. Above all, write 'English as she is spoke'.

Here's my submission for bettering the 'Pre-Qualification – Commercial Catering Equipment' letter:

Dear Sirs

What do you or your clients look for from a new catering installation – be it a kitchen, a complete restaurant or whatever?

We would suggest:
- the very best equipment
- the most efficient equipment
- at the most equitable cost.

And after the installation
- the longest maintenance free life
- the minimum possible running costs.

Can we give you all this? It is quite likely. Being part of the ... group we have probably acquired more know-how (UK and internationally) than most quality suppliers. Our corporate purchasing power enables us to match anyone on price while maintaining top quality, and, when it matters, to acquire equipment faster.

We are also innovators – often the first to introduce new ideas, new applications and new equipment, but always thoroughly testing the innovation within our group's many hotels and restaurants before adding it to our portfolio.

Can we come and talk to you? Show you some of the projects we have worked on and some of the operating figures and publicity that our installations have subsequently achieved?

We will telephone in about one week's time to arrange a firm appointment. Meanwhile, if anything is currently 'cooking' do not hesitate to ring us.

Yours faithfully

If you're Managing Sales ...

Go through all your standard selling letters. Re-write anything that doesn't fit your chosen Corporate Image. (You should re-write all your standard letters every three months, anyway!) Brief your typists, secretaries and executives on the changes in objective, format, and on AIDA. Do it today or tomorrow. Any delay is costing you business. Your competitors may be reading this, too.

Remember that old TV series, 'Never Mind the Quality, Feel the Width'? When it comes to quality sales literature, it is pretty near the truth. Apart from colour and type styles and decent pictures (preferably but not essentially colour) the key two factors which make sales literature top quality are:

- the thickness, smoothness, colour, texture and feel of the paper or board used

- the words, the prose, the 'poetry' put into the explanations, descriptions, 'picture-painting'.

Never penny pinch on the paper quality. If you do, you'll lose. Go up in thickness every time, if in doubt. Collect samples, always have dummies prepared by your printers so that you can get the true 'feel', and always thoroughly proof-read your copy, with all the pictures, graphs and columns of figures where they should be.

If your company cars, delivery vans, lorries, service estate cars and whatever else you use aren't kept clean, aren't properly sign-written under the same rules I've already mentioned for advertising, and aren't the most appropriate colours for your chosen position in the Quality league table – you'll down-grade yourself yet again.

Most companies allow their salesforce to choose the colour of their cars. Other companies don't care what colour their cars are, as long as they've got four wheels and an engine. Both wrong.

If you have a quality house colour, try to match it up on everything. If that isn't possible for cars because it's a special, pick a colour that is complementary to your house colour so that you have a quality colour combination. It doesn't cost any more to get this right. Think what the cigarette firms do with their company cars.

Never use those vacuum-formed plastic stick-on signs for the sides of your delivery vans and lorries. If you want to portray the Corporate Image of a temporary supplier that won't be in business next week, this is as good a way as any. And when the sign-writing on your vans starts getting worn and thin, so that it's difficult to read completely – have it done again, fast. You must have followed many vans and lorries that look like this. Remember what you thought about it at the time? Then think about why Eddie Stobart has a fan club. Always clean. All 800. And every driver wears a tie.

If you want the worst combination for a quality corporate image, try worn sign-writing, an unwashed vehicle and rust!

The way you present your proposals, your quotations, your offer, is critically important in many ways, not the least of which is your enhanced position in the Quality league table.

Are your proposals packaged in a professional looking quality binder or folder? Is the paper they are typed and printed on as good as the paper you use for your quality sales literature and selling letters? Are the colours right? Do you take the important ones in and present them properly, rather than simply stick them in the post?

Is there anything you include in your proposals that sticks out like a sore thumb? The odd piece of cheaply duplicated specification or servicing instructions amongst the quality paperwork. If there is, dig it out and do it properly on decent paper.

The best example I've ever seen of a really quality proposal was by Coventry-based fighting vehicle manufacturers Alvis Ltd. They were going for a £15 million order for Saracen troop carriers from the Saudi Arabian Government. Okay, when you've the potential profit from £15 million to play with, you can push the boat out a bit with your proposals, but this one was still exceptional, notwithstanding this advantage, and what Alvis did can be emulated at very low cost by most businesses.

There were 12 people on the Government's buying team, headed by the Commander of the National Guard, who was also a member of the Saudi Royal Family. Thus, Alvis prepared 12 copies of its proposals, plus a few more, just in case. And the copies were top copies. No photocopies. Each copy of the proposals was bound into a white, grained plastic, padded front ring binder. (If you want to do business with the Middle East, be *very* careful with colours. White is by far the best.)

On the front face of each white binder, the name of the recipient, the individual member of the Government's team, was printed in gold leaf. The one for the team's leader, a copy of which is one of my treasured possessions, reads:

ALVIS LTD

PROPOSAL
RELATED TO WHEELED ARMOURED VEHICLES
for
H.R.H. ABDULLAH BIN ABDUL AZIZ
COMMANDER NATIONAL GUARD

ALVIS LTD, COVENTRY, ENGLAND

Inside the binder, as well as all the technical and commercial information, was a full colour picture of a squadron of Saracen troop carriers travelling fast across the desert. A well-known artist had been commissioned to paint, in oils, the original picture, which had then been given to Alvis's printers, to be used as artwork for a run of just fifty full colour prints on top quality art paper. The Saudi Government team was very impressed with this artist's impression of what their new troop carriers would look like travelling across the Saudi Arabian desert.

The team leader was even more impressed when, at an appropriate time during Alvis's presentation of its proposals, he was personally presented with the original oil painting, in a most gorgeous intricately gilded frame, by Alvis's Managing Director.

Who could lose when this much trouble was taken? Alvis certainly didn't. Original oil paintings may be stretching things a bit for *your* proposals – but individual gold blocking and top quality binders aren't. The gold blocking would cost you around £5 to £10 a binder. The binder itself less than £5.

'HOW MUCH?' the prospective customer's eyebrows rise as much as his voice.
There you are, well on the way to selling him this top quality merchandise, his objectives clearly defined, his doubts about its performance, life, market reputation and your company's ditto all professionally handled, you thought, to his complete satisfaction. Quantities established. Starting dates provisionally considered. And now this. The usual thorny problem. Time and again, just when everything is going well, the customer goes and ruins it all with those two terrible words.

Your inner self starts sweating again. It sees an attack of 'Price Fright' coming on. It hasn't yet realised fully that because you are now a *positive* and have bags of confidence that has come from all the extra knowledge you've been acquiring since you picked up these books, things are changing.

Now you're beginning to feel proud of your prices – because you know in detail how and why they are justified. But maybe your inner self isn't so sure that customers realize this. After all, if they did, if you were *really* putting the benefits and the justification over properly, they wouldn't keep shouting 'How much?' at you so often, would they?

Yes, they would. It makes no difference how good you are at presenting your case – the customer has *his* job to do, and part of that job is to get the best possible products and services for the lowest possible price.

He's going to test you on price, whatever and however you do. He's going to see how firm you're going to be. He's going to watch your reaction to his *'How much?'* and gauge, in his own mind, the kind of reduction or discount you're likely to give him.

Play poker with him. With complete sincerity. Without flinching. Without batting an eyelid.

'Don't you think the quality, the performance, the longer life, the lower servicing cost, the extra demand we've been discussing, is *worth* that much, Mr Dobson?'

If he splutters, hedges, laughs or plays poker back at you with something like, 'That's not the point,' you can continue: 'Just like any business that puts quality first, as, I suspect, yours does, if we didn't maintain our margins, we wouldn't be able to maintain our quality for very long, either. It's a fair price for the value you'll be getting, don't you think?'

If it's an average test, he's likely to give up about there. If he's a man of principle, he might persist a while longer. 'No, it's too expensive.'

''When you say it's too expensive, do you mean you can't afford to pay our price? Is there something I've missed?' or 'Do you mean you don't feel this is going to be an economical proposition for your company?'

Depending on the reply you get to this, you might continue: 'How much too expensive do you feel we are?' or 'How much more is this than you wanted to spend?'

You are seeking to establish the difference between your price and what he sees as reasonable.

You must define the difference. This is absolutely critical. Then, when you know how much or how little he is worrying about, you go back to your bag of justification benefits and you reduce the difference to the lowest common denominator.

Say you are selling something that has a working life of five years and the difference he's worrying about is £130. That's 50p a week for 260 weeks. Or 7p a day.

'Isn't getting the best *worth* an extra 50p a week, Mr Dobson?'

Another way of dealing with 'It's too expensive' is to ask back: 'In relation to what?' and see which way he goes. You'll get a specific objection with which you can easily deal.

Then you can back it up with: 'Let's face it Mr Dobson, you're not interested in *raw cost* – you're interested in *value for money* aren't you? I think I've shown that you will get the best possible value for money if you buy from us. You get this, and this, and this, and you get *me*. Being the best goes right across our company.'

Normally, if you are progressing up the Quality league table, your price will also progressively rise. That Perceived Value factor will look after your profit margins. Of course, if you are happy with your profit margins and you can rise up the Quality league table at very little extra cost, you can afford to hold your prices down and take a significantly larger share of the market. But don't hold your prices down too much, otherwise cognitive dissonance will set in and the customers won't believe you can be that good with prices that low. Keep the balance right.

Up against competition, your customer, considering the four or five quotations he's received, might say to you, 'You are the most expensive!' You'll get the utmost satisfaction from saying, 'Yes, we are' and then saying nothing for four or five seconds. It's amazing how many customers will then say to you, 'I suppose that's because you're the best.' To which you reply, 'Yes – absolutely right'.

If you find yourself up against just one competitor and that competitor is down at the bottom of the Quality league table, the customer might say, 'You're a lot more expensive than …

There is an awful temptation to knock the competition here. Don't do it. You can get the point over by inference without anyone laying a knock at your door. Sell the difference.

'Yes, we are a lot more expensive. But let me ask you a question.

Isn't it true that in every kind of business, there are companies that provide a service that does as much as possible for their customers and there are companies that provide a service which does just enough for them to get by with?'

'Yes, I suppose that's true' says the customer.

'Well, what would you like us to do for you – as much as possible or just enough to get by with?'

If you can devise a simple sales aid – a visual aid – to help you overcome the 'How much' merchants, this always makes justifying your higher price much easier.

Here's one for capital equipment salespeople at the top end of the market.

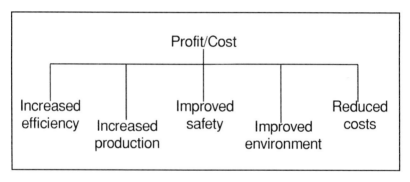

The customer has said, 'You're a lot more expensive than your competitors.' The salesperson brings out his **Profit/Cost chart** and says, 'Yes, we are. But this isn't going to be very relevant to you. You see, if I've done my sums correctly, you're not going to spend a penny in real terms.' He points to his chart. 'Because of how our equipment is going to increase your efficiency, your production, improve your safety, your working conditions *and* reduce your production and stocking costs – and we can quantify every one of these – you're going to show a profit almost from day one.

'With us you'll be buying the best. So your profit will be greater than if you bought from our competitors, and you'll be getting that profit for a longer period of time.'

The most effective way of all to deal with problems on Price is to scotch them all – right at the *beginning* of your presentation. Here is a technique I put together for a double glazing company. The salespeople dealt with husbands and wives in the home.

Just 10 minutes into the first discussion, during the initial tour of the house or browse through the range of products, it doesn't matter which, the salesperson says to his prospective customers, 'Before we go any further, rather than waste your time, can I ask you a question? When you buy things for your home, especially things that have to last a long time, do you shop around for the cheapest thing you can buy, or do you look for best value for money?'

The only answer anyone is going to get to that question is, 'Oh, we look for best value for money, of course'. Even if it isn't true, no one is going to admit to being a cheapjack. Their egos would never let them.

'Good,' continues the salesperson, 'because that's precisely what my company stands for – Best Value for Money. We aren't the cheapest, and we aren't the most expensive either, but we are the best.'

Then, a switch to phase two of this technique.

'Hey, I was talking to someone in this area only the other day who has exactly the same view of the importance of going for best value for money as you do. You might know him. What was his name? *(Think, then search in pockets.)* Hang on, he gave me his card. I've got it here somewhere. I remember, it had something printed on the back I thought summed our business up beautifully. Ah, here it is.'

The salesperson pulls out a business card and reads out the name of the person printed on the front. 'George Thomson. Do you know him?' Then he turns the card over… 'How about this?'… and reads the quotation printed on the card.

When he's read the quotation completely to his prospective customers, the salesperson says 'Nothing's new, is it? 1819 to 1900. A hundred years ago and people were just the same as they are now.' Then he hands the card to the husband and says, 'Here, you have it. One of your friends might know him.'

Both husband and wife will read the quotation again, during which time the salesperson keeps quiet. After that, no problems with price, as long as the customers can *afford* the double glazing, of course.

Value ...

It's unwise to pay too much, but it's unwise to pay too little. When you pay too much you lose a little money, that is all.

When you pay too little, you sometimes lose everything because the thing you bought was incapable of doing the thing you bought it to do. The common law of business balance prohibits paying a little and getting a lot. It can't be done. If you deal with the lowest bidder, it's well to add something for the risk you run.

And if you do that, you will have enough to pay for something better.

John Ruskin (1819-1900)

You can simplify this technique by printing the John Ruskin quotation on the back of your *own* business card, and also having it in your literature, but that's not as effective as having it on someone else's card.

The oldest and still very effective method of justifying a higher price uses the four arithmetic symbols:

$$+ \quad - \quad \div \quad \times$$

Add ... all the benefits of the higher-priced product or service.

Take away ... what the customer will lose by not buying the higher-priced product.

Divide ... the cost by time or by other parameters.

Multiply ... the savings or gains over the life of the higher-priced product.

That's Selling Quality!

Do you reckon your prices are too high? If so, why do you think they are too high? In relation to what? So how do your 'extras' compare with your competitors? If you don't know, you need a day's worth of USP (covered in Chapter 8 xx).

Here's another interesting factor. Quite a few customers who say to you, 'It's too expensive' or 'It costs too much' are lying to you. They're saying that because they don't want to tell you their real problem.

The customer who's got into financial difficulties because of his own bad management isn't going to admit this to you and say, 'I can't afford to buy your goods just now'. He's going to say, 'They cost too much'.

The customer who bought too much last month and is stuck with a warehouse full of slow-moving products isn't going to say to you, 'First I have to make some space in my warehouse'. He's going to say, 'They are too expensive'.

The cut-price customer who has a reputation for only selling the cheapest products isn't going to say, 'My own style has made it impossible for me to handle your quality goods'. He's going to say, 'My word, they're too expensive'.

The customer whose company has a turnover much smaller than its PR department has been making out recently, isn't going to say to you, 'We haven't got enough work for this machine for it to earn its keep'. He's going to say (all together now) *'It's too expensive!'*

So question it – every time.

'What do you really mean when you say it's too expensive?'

Don't *ever* accept it. Not the first time, not the second time, not even the third time. You're not selling prices; you're selling *quality, value, lower costs, longer life, satisfaction, safety, peace of mind*, and a hundred other things for which it's worth paying a *higher price*.

Now a thought or two for those salespeople who sell to retailers.

Retailers should not be over-concerned about price, unless it is their concern to make sure they are selling the highest-priced goods they can safely move.

Retailers should be concerned with:

1   **Volume** – the number of units he can sell in a given time ... and

2   **Profit** – the money he makes every time he sells one unit.

If the retailers sell the highest-priced units, they will logically make the most profit on each unit. They should know this (some retailers don't seem to), but their fears are focused on moving their stock. If they stock too much high-priced merchandise, will they get stuck with it if their customers choose to go for the cheaper brands?

Salespeople therefore have to dispel the retailer's fears by talking about how effective their company's forthcoming advertising campaigns will be in stimulating consumer demand in this area. And how their company is going to back-up the retailer with point-of-sale displays so as to make sure the retailer's stocks move fast.

And at the same time the salespeople tickle the retailer's greed taste-buds with projections for a year based on a higher profit per unit multiplied by the number of units they expect the retailer to sell in a year.

If it's a high-priced piece of equipment that needs servicing and the retailers are responsible for the servicing because of the prevailing trend for manufacturers to pass this buck down the line as far as they can go, then the salespeople have an additional arrow to fire.

The cost of the servicing comes out of the retailers' profit. The more units they sell, the more servicing costs and servicing 'aggro' they get. Logically, the higher the price of the unit, the more reliable it is, and the less the retailers' servicing costs per unit anyway.

So let's make up a set of calculations for our retail salesperson to use:

The retailer is currently buying XYZ equipment at £200 per unit. His servicing cost per year averages £20 per unit. His gross profit per unit is £70. He currently sells 150 units per year. Thus his net profit per year is £50 x 150 = £7,500.

The sales proposal is that the retailer switches to the more expensive ABC equipment at £300 per unit. Servicing costs per year will average £10 per unit. The gross profit per unit will be £110. The salesperson estimates the retailer will sell 100 units per year. Thus his projected net profit will be £100 x 100 = £10,000, with fewer selling problems.

Of course, it will rarely be a clear-cut case of switching from one product to another. No retailer will risk an all-or-nothing situation.

Unit ABC will be introduced alongside unit XYZ and, if the salesperson's estimates are proven in the ensuing year, the XYZ units will be steadily phased out or down to a minimum level consistent with consumer demand.

Whichever way the salesperson plays it, faced with these profit projections, most retailers are going to remain doubtful. But this final doubt is just what the salesperson needs for a cast-iron, certain 'try it for size' close:

> 'Look, I can see you're still not sure. Why don't we go for half this quantity for the first quarter? Then, if my projections are right, you can double-up from the second quarter onwards. That way you've got to be safe.'

Sold!

Finally, let's look at a different kind of 'How much?' reaction from the prospective customers. The kind who don't react violently to your high price – they sit there calmly and say, 'Can I have a discount?'

It's another way the customers try to do their job – best value for money; lowest price!

Look worried. Frown for a few seconds. Slowly shake your head and say:

> 'Oh dear. That does give us a problem. You see, we don't give our old-established, very large customers a discount. What do you think they'd think of us if they found out we'd given you one?'
>
> If he smiles and says, 'Don't worry, I won't tell them!' you keep going with:
>
> 'That's not the point really, is it? It's simply not our policy to give discounts. We aim to offer best value for money, best service, best quality, best reliability, longest life. To be able to do that, we must protect our margins.'

Stick to your guns. He's getting a bargain, really. You know that. All you've got to do is convince him.

43

Often, top quality suppliers take longer to deliver than cheap and cheerful suppliers. If your delivery is shorter than your lesser quality competitors, great. Turn to the next piece of the puzzle. If your delivery is longer than you feel it should be to compete, read on.

Why is your delivery longer? 'Because so many forward-looking customers want to buy from us.'

If this were a fast food restaurant, you'd be in and out in ten minutes. But it's not; it's a top quality restaurant. There's something printed on the bottom of the menu: 'Good food takes time to prepare – please be patient'.

'Quality is worth waiting for.' That's what you've got to get over to the customer who wants delivery *now!* In his mind, time is the essence. A sense of urgency is in the air. You need to change the most important factor in his mind from time to *quality.*

'I can appreciate that delivery seems vital to you at this stage, but surely, in the long run, the fact that you are ordering the best equipment must be the deciding factor?'

If you're in trouble because of a *past* delivery problem, try this one.

The customer's saying to you: 'That widget crusher we bought from you a year ago. It was seven weeks late. It cost us thousands. We decided then – never again.'

'I can understand that but let me ask you – if you were running a business where products were going out seven weeks late, what would you do about it?'

You might not get the answer you want, but, then again, you might. If you do, you then say:

'That's precisely (or more or less) what we did,' and you tell the customer in detail. After that, your troubles are either little ones or over.

If you find out you're going to be late on delivery, before it actually happens, telephone the customer fast and tell him. Burying your head in the sand and hoping the problem will blow away is not for Quality league leaders, only for cheap and cheerfuls.

 The packaging of your product is not just so much waste paper, board and polystyrene chunks. The packaging is the first glimpse of your product that many customers see. If the packaging is rubbish, cheap, badly put together, the best product in the world will come out of it with a much lower Perceived Value.

They'll maybe buy once, but what about the second time, and all the people they talk to?

Don't skimp on your packaging. Make it earn business for you. It's part of your sales promotion, just like the sides of your delivery vehicles. What's wrong with printing your guarantee on the outside of the packaging in big bold letters? What's wrong with printing some of your more choice Selling Quality headlines, from your sales literature, on your packaging?

Like Hartmann Luggage:

ENJOY IT –
YOU HAVE BOUGHT THE BEST

Like Rank Xerox for the 'Diplomat Copier':

THE COPIER YOU WON'T
WANT TO HIDE IN A CORNER

Don't forget to get the colours right again. It's still important.

If your product is bought in retail stores and you want to persuade browsing prospective customers to pay a little more and buy something which will last a lot longer, maybe your packaging should have added to it a 'Share Certificate'.

INVESTMENT
1,000 SHARES

With Inflation likely to rise and the Economy soft, an investment in a top quality product is a necessity in all your personal purchases.

A top quality product will last longer. It won't break down or wear out as fast, giving you an investment in enduring quality.

45

A top quality product never goes out of style.

By spending a little more now, you'll avoid repeating your purchase soon because it wore out or went out of style. This means real savings in the long run.

Make that investment now and get as a dividend the only full warranty 18-month guarantee in the industry, backed by the oldest and most reliable company in the industry.

INVEST IN A
HARTMANN

 Your back-up starts with the switchboard operator and receptionist and goes right through the organisation and up to the Managing Director. *No one* is excluded. Rank Audio Visual produced a superb training video some years ago, which has never been bettered for getting across to every employee the importance of the customer and the importance of providing the right kind of back-up. The video is called *'Who Killed the Sale?'* Show it to all your people, including the Managing Director, once every three months. Video Arts also has a superb training video for resolving back-up problems, featuring John Cleese and Ronnie Barker, called *'It's All Right, It's Only a Customer!'* Both titles portray the complete message!

Take note:

You never get a second chance to make a
FIRST IMPRESSION

Remember 'Think a Smile' for incoming calls to the sales office? Well, 'Think a Smile' begins with the company's switchboard operator. Where *do* they find these girls? It's as if they were selected for the most depressing voices and for how long they can hold their breath before answering a call!

If you want to be top on Quality, you've got to get these kind of things right and *keep* them right. One bad day and you lose. And you'll never know what you lost; that's the problem. Out of sight, out of mind, so you don't worry enough about this perpetual problem area.

To illustrate what kind of back-up you need for Selling Quality, turn to Chapter 2, where I take you through what *should* happen when a prospective customer visits your company for what I call a **conducted tour of the works.**

 Selling is the most important job in the world. That's where we began. Service – servicing the products that you've sold or performing the service you've sold – is the *second* most important job. Get the Service wrong, and you don't have any repeat business. Worse than that, your unhappy customers tell their friends and then you don't have as much new business, either.

The very first training video that Video Arts ever made featured John Cleese and was titled, '*Who Sold You This Then?*' John Cleese is Charlie Jenkins, current world record holder as a service engineer, for *un-selling* more customers than anyone else. He runs down the product, he runs down his company, he runs down the customer and he runs down the salesperson who sold the product he is servicing. As a result, customers run shrieking into the night.

Everyone who sees that video laughs their socks off – except service engineers. They hardly ever laugh. You see, the film leaves them nowhere to go, because, the world over, service engineers are like Charlie Jenkins.

If you want to aspire to a higher level in the Quality league table, or if you simply want to win and keep more business away from your competitors, you've got to make your service people more professional than the vast majority.

In fmcg markets (fast moving consumer goods) the service people are already highly professional, however. For businesses that sell to retail stores, service is called Merchandising, and merchandisers are responsible for making sure that their company's products are properly and prominently displayed, that the point-of-sale material, provided by their company, is in good condition, dusted regularly and replaced where necessary. They have an on-going objective, which is steadily to get a bit more shelf space for their company's products, every time they visit the retailer.

To achieve all this, a merchandiser is very thoroughly trained, and this training is very near to the training any salesperson should receive.

And here lies the key to why service engineers of the industrial and domestic variety are so bad. The training *they* receive is on how to service the product. Very rarely indeed do these kind of service engineers receive training in Selling, or customer liaison, or basic communication, or even 'why we are in business!'

So if you really want to sell Quality, that's what you do first. Train your service people as if they were SALESpeople.

Because they are!

They get opportunities to sell that the salespeople themselves rarely, if ever, get. Customers, if the service engineers are really good, look upon them as impartial experts. Yes, impartial! Customers listen when these kinds of service engineers recommend that a certain piece of equipment should be replaced, or that a certain competitor's product should be phased out in favour of their own company's MK4YB. If the service engineers can justify, as a salesperson has to justify, their recommendation with figures and proof, the customers will do what they recommend. Or they may alternatively set up a meeting between the customers and their colleague in the salesforce, so that the salespeople take over to clinch the deal.

That's another thing about really professional service engineers – they work very closely with their salespeople. The service force and the salesforce have regular meetings together, for training and for planning campaigns. Responsibility for service and for sales is carried by one senior executive in the best run Selling Quality companies. Where service is the responsibility of Production, warring tribes usually exist and the company plays straight into a more professional competitor's hands.

Service engineers are exceedingly well placed to sell spare parts, replacement units, maintenance contracts, as well as to advise the customers and their company's sales department on opportunities to sell. A well-tuned service force can generate as many leads as a well-planned advertising campaign. Service engineers can quite easily, when trained, use end-of-call question techniques. 'By the way, before I go, do you know anyone else in this area who could use this kind of equipment?' or 'By the way, before I go, Mrs Brown, could any of your friends in this neighbourhood do with a new washing machine?'

Service engineers who regularly look after postal franking machines are trained to watch for increases in usage of their machines. When usage reaches a certain level, they begin talking to the customer on their servicing visits about the imminent need for a larger machine. Then they set up a visit for their salesforce, who come in and sell the larger machine. Photocopier and word-processor maintenance engineers do likewise. Many local word-processor engineers carry new machines in their cars and can effect on-the-spot sales with no one else needing to get involved.

Now what can I say about motor dealer service receptions, where you take your car for its regular 5,000 mile service, or for a repair? We all know the trauma we go through in this particular industry. They are diabolically bad. It's absurdly easy to change all that – and make service reception a profit centre in its own right. A few drivers and a good quality mail shot letter is all you need. You've already got the necessary cars.

Dear Customer

As from 1 March you don't have to bring your car to our service reception in Main Road any more for your regular service or a repair.

No more waiting. No more wasting your time twice in the same day. From 1 March we will collect your car from your home or place of business and return it to either.

At a time agreed with you, one of our experienced drivers will establish in detail your requirements for the service/repair and will bring your car to our service department. At the end of the day, again at a time agreed with you, the same driver will return your car. If you have an account with us, that's all there is to it; we'll invoice you as usual. If you're a cash customer, our driver will have the invoice with him and will accept your cheque.

There will be a small charge for this collection and delivery service, but we are sure you will find that, compared with the loss of your time, the charge is more than acceptable.

When you are ready for your next service, please ring the number below. From our records this should be around ...

If you would rather continue to bring your car to us and collect it from us, as you have done in the past, then of course you can do this. Simply ignore this letter and we look forward to seeing you next time you are at Main Road. (By the way, we've now installed a coffee machine for our customers in our service reception.)'

Only penny-pinching customers will be reluctant to take advantage of this new collection service. Only they will henceforth witness the trauma and hassle in service reception on a busy morning or evening. All the *good* customers, and certainly all the business customers, will be oblivious of any problems and will be telling their friends and colleagues about this 'different' motor dealer.

One motor dealership I know has gone one better than even this. It offers its business customers a **'Night shift service'** collecting the car for service after 6.00pm in the evening and delivering it back to the customer's front door by 7.30am the next morning.

If you actually sell a service, rather than a product, then your service people are the people who perform the service you sell. All I have said applies equally to them.

And throughout the service function, your people need to look and behave as up-market as the salespeople do in their piece of the Quality jigsaw puzzle. The service engineer's paperwork is just as important as the salesperson's – in the eyes of the customers. Make it as professional as you can.

And now a word on the bit that comes between delivery of the product and its first service – the **operating instructions.**

It's a fact of life that every set of operating instructions says in bold type **'Read these instructions carefully before you touch the product'.**

It's also a fact of life that very few customers ever *do* read the instructions. So you get more early failures or malfunctions than you should get and instant dissatisfied customers. Cracking this problem can save you a lot of money, enhance your product's perceived value and bring you new customers. Here are a few suggestions:

1   Make your operating instructions a sales brochure. Put some good action pictures in it - a few happy customers using the product, with quotes.

2   Print your instructions in big type, not small, hard-to-read type, and on good quality paper. Never duplicate or photocopy. Have plenty of good diagrams. Use colour. In other words, make the operating instructions look and feel important, expensive and interesting.

3   Have a really big main heading on the front of your instructions, which hits the customer right between the eyes Something like:

    'Our competitors tell us their customers never read their operating instructions. Maybe that's why our customers get so much more pleasure out of their ...'

    Or, if you want to challenge the customer.

    'If this product were a sports car, these operating instructions would enable you to do 0-60 in 5 seconds on your first run. Without them, you'd probably do 0-30 in 3 hours!'

Finally, for this Service jigsaw piece, how do you *tell* the prospective customers about your incredibly good service back-up? I'm sure you don't make the mistake one manufacturer made a few years back. In the sales literature it said:

Our equipment is utterly reliable and never goes wrong, but when it does ... we'll have a service engineer at your door within 48 hours.

One of the best examples I've seen of putting over Service on paper is this:

Service you can RELY on

1600 engineers in a nationwide network ensure that Rank Xerox delivers quality, reliability and service.

Choose a Rank Xerox copier or duplicator for your office and you're not just getting an advanced product. You'll also be gaining access to the most comprehensive copier and duplicator service network in the country - service you can depend on, whether you rent, lease or buy.

Service has always been a Rank Xerox priority. Wherever you are, we're not too far away. And we get to you fast when you need us.

The Success of the 'Diplomat'

A few years ago, Rank Xerox put into practice most of what I've said in this chapter. They did it as a test case for one product only, a 'limited edition' of their proven and very successful plain paper copier, the 3100. They called their limited edition the *Diplomat.*

It was an aesthetically delightful combination of top quality colours – beige, dark brown and black; a modern single tubular column chromed stand with cruciform base and four rubber-tyred castors with chromed brakes; a streamlined, slimmed down copier unit and, to set everything off, delicate brown and black coach lines on the beige paintwork and a Royal Warrant, the Queen's coat of arms and 'By appointment to Her Majesty the Queen',

The sales brochure produced to launch the Diplomat was equally different and impressive. Not large, A5 in fact, half as big as Rank Xerox's normal sales literature, but on very good quality board and printed full colour, the background colours setting off the pictures of the Diplomat to perfection. Plenty of plant life, cork wall tiles, that kind of thing.

The headline read:

The Xerox 3100 Diplomat.
Makes every other plain paper copier ... look plain.

The internal copy read:

Why settle for an ordinary plain paper copier when you can have a Xerox 3100 Diplomat – the exciting new copier with proven efficiency and good looks.

(I'm going to give you the entire text, because, like the Rolls-Royce Shadow I brochure, there is so much to learn from this example.)

The copier you won't want to hide in a corner.

Your own design sense will instantly tell you that here, at last, is a copier that looks as impressive as its performance.

The Xerox 3100 Diplomat is an efficient, functional piece of office equipment that's also smart enough to be the office showpiece. Whether it sits in reception, the MD's office or the typing pool.

Wherever you place it, it never looks out of place.

Where the space is at a premium, the Xerox 3100 Diplomat can actually contribute to the go-ahead, modern look of the working environment. It not only embodies the kind of style that appeals to every interior decorator's eye: it incorporates the business efficiency functions, reliability and service back-up you insist upon.

It's image-conscious – and ruthlessly cost-conscious, too.

The Xerox 3100 Diplomat is compact, completely portable and your accountant will approve of it for all the right economic reasons. Its pedigree is the world-renowned Xerox 3100 series, one of the most relied-upon low volume copiers in the business.

The name Rank Xerox speaks volumes about the efficiency of the Diplomat. Its impeccable styling means that now you can have a copier that also reflects your company's image.

Good-looking, hard-working, easy-to-operate.

20 copies a minute. First copy time eight seconds. The ability to copy virtually any original on to practically any material. Two-way light/dark copy switch to improve the quality of poor originals. One quick automatic cycle for copying and paperfeeding. At a glance paper renewal display. All features designed to speed up the efficiency process.

Lease or buy...

And at the same time, enjoy one of the most efficient back-up services in the country.

There are over 1,600 Service Engineers operating through a network of Service Centres, dedicated to keeping your Xerox equipment at the peak of efficiency.

Tear off and post the Reply Paid Card now for details.

This is a 'special edition' copier – and if you want the chance to obtain one at an equally attractive price – please hurry. Fill in and post the card. Now – while the image of this not-so-plain paper copier is still fresh in your mind.

The Diplomat was outstandingly successful. It hadn't got the storage cupboard that the standard 3100 copier was supplied with, but the customers didn't mind that. It hadn't got the second paper tray that the standard 3100 had, but the customers didn't mind that either. They were buying style. They liked the look of the Diplomat and were prepared to pay more for it - £410 more to be precise. During its last few months on the market, the Diplomat was selling for £1,925, against the standard 3100 copier at £1,515.

That's really Selling Quality.

Well, that's a sample dozen jigsaw puzzle pieces plus one complete example of how to put it all together. All you need to do now is decide how many pieces your particular Corporate Image jigsaw puzzle has, and what each piece is labelled, because every business is different. The 12 pieces I've selected are probably the most universally common pieces, but there are many more. How do you establish which pieces you need?

Try getting your people together for a day's worth of USP. The results will show you clearly what your edge is over your competitors, for each of your products and markets. If your edge on any particular factor is not very bright, or if your competitors are beating you on that factor, you have a potential piece for your jigsaw puzzle.

You will also be able to quantify each piece. How much improvement you need for just the right amount of edge. There's no point in having too much on some pieces and not enough on others.

Every Demonstration has an objective, usually to prove to a customer that what the Salesperson says will happen does happen.

But Demonstrations can come in all shapes and sizes. Some are very different from others – and much more successful because of it.

Our Demonstrations must help us to win – so they're going to be very different from those of our competitors.

Chapter 2

How to Demonstrate Your Superiority

Why is it so many demonstrations go wrong? Here we are, caught up in the spiral of the fastest expanding industry of the New Millennium – Information Technology. Hardware and software salespeople are coming out of the woodwork everywhere. And more times than not, the demonstration you get of the latest, or past latest, system leaves you wondering why you ever wanted to discard that lever arch filing system.

Before that it was photocopiers. How many people in business *have not* been subjected to a photocopier demonstration that went wrong?

Whenever an industry booms, so that salesforces expand so rapidly the training of those salesforces can't keep up with the recruitment rate, your demonstrations are the first things to suffer.

The people conducting the demonstrations haven't been taught enough about the product in general, or about the art of conducting a good demonstration in particular. Yet we all know, with absolute certainty, that if a product demonstration goes wrong, the sale is *lost*. Irretrievably lost. Forever. *And* that prospective customer talks about it to friends.

Commercial suicide is being committed every day by businesses everywhere that really know better, and should be doing better.

Then there's the other kind of 'demonstration'. The salesperson picks up the customer from his premises at around 11.45am. They drive straight to the salesperson's favourite top class restaurant.

An hour in the bar and then they roll into the dining room. Two bottles of vino over the lunch, two double brandies over the coffee and by 3pm they're ready for the demonstration. Short drive to the works, 10 minutes talking about the product and the prospective customer looks at his watch and says, 'I've got to get back to sign the post!'

I know salespeople who have lost their driving licence, and the order, trying to get the prospective customer back to base in a hurry after this kind of 'demonstration'. And why bother? Let's face it, if the objective of the exercise is to get the customer well and truly tipsy at your expense, you can do it much more effectively if you didn't have a demonstration to get in the way of progress!

If you want to win against serious competition, your demonstrations have got to go right, not wrong. Every time. And that needs systematic planning, preparation and technique. It also needs the active co-operation of quite a few other people.

Here are the rules.

The Objectives

Once you have committed yourself and your prospective customer to a demonstration, sit down alone with your A4 survey pad and list the objectives on paper. Why are you conducting this demonstration? What specific doubts do you need to dispel from the prospective customer's mind? How can you best dispel these doubts? What other things could you demonstrate which would enhance the customer's appreciation of your product and your company's prowess, without detracting from the key objectives that you *must* achieve?

Now that you have this information on paper, you can begin planning and preparing for the demonstration.

The Administration

Still with your survey pad, make a second list. What will be required to achieve the objectives? Where would be the best place to hold the demonstration? When? Who will be attending from the customer company? Who will be required from your company, other than you? What literature and samples will be needed? Will any food and drink be required during the time the customer is in your hands?

Now you can get to work and tie all the pieces together. Memos to any of the company's staff from whom you need assistance. Requisitions for the appropriate equipment. Firm booking of your demonstration unit if the demonstration is to be conducted on your premises or on the prospective customer's premises. Telephone your old established customer and make sure the date is convenient, if the demonstration is to be held at another customer's premises. Which brings me to the third very critical point.

Check up beforehand

This is absolutely essential if you plan to conduct demonstrations at your customer's premises, using their product, which you sold them a year ago and with which as far as you know, they're very happy.

Don't, under any circumstances, rely on just the telephone call when you agreed the date and time. Visit those customers personally beforehand to make sure everything is okay, that your products will be being used on the day in question, that they will be used by competent people. Brief that person on why you are bringing this prospective customer to see this particular equipment, and what you need to have demonstrated to that customer, and why again. Come over to those people in a way that makes that demonstration and the responsibility you've delegated the most important thing in their life as well as yours. Fuss over them. Ask them if they need anything from you to make their charge perform like it's never performed before.

I know one very successful machine tool sales engineer who carries a few spare control wheels and levers in the boot of his car, ready for just such situations. He knows from experience that the operators of his machine tools don't use the machine's wheels and levers as they should be used, they take a copper hammer and hit them every few seconds to clamp components tight or to reset tooling. It's faster for the operators, easier on the muscles, and does the machine no harm. But after a few months, it makes the wheels and levers look a mess. Scars and dents in the satin chrome finish. Spoils the overall aesthetics of his product.

So the day before a demonstration, the sales engineer visits the customer, checks out everything, briefs the machine operator, and changes the wheels and levers for new ones, making the operator promise that he won't use his copper hammer until after the old wheels and levers have been replaced, the day after the demonstration.

This so impresses the operator, the sales engineer claims, that he sometimes goes to the trouble of turning up to work for the day of the demonstration in freshly cleaned and pressed overalls, hair cut, shaved properly that morning, all the junk has been cleared away from around the machine and the machine itself performs 20 per cent faster than it does in normal production.

He's the only one in his salesforce who takes that kind of trouble to get things right, and he's top of the sales league table consistently.

I was privy to a demonstration a few years ago where the salesman didn't check up beforehand. I was one of three prospective customers looking at a particular piece of office equipment. We arrived at the customer's premises, were introduced to the commercial manager, who escorted us to the piece of equipment we'd come to see. I wondered at the time why the commercial manager seemed a touch distant and tight lipped.

When we reached the salesman's equipment, he exclaimed in surprise, 'It's not working!' The commercial manager just looked at him and said quietly, 'No. It hasn't worked for a week. And can we get one of your service engineers out here – can we hell!' And he walked away and left us standing there.

The salesman couldn't understand why I couldn't stop laughing. The customer got his service engineer within the hour, but it didn't do the salesman much good. He still lost three potential orders and the goodwill of that existing customer, whom he certainly couldn't use for a demonstration ever again.

Do check up beforehand – personally.

The demonstration itself

During the demonstration itself, there is a specific format you should try to follow. It's called 'TELL – SHOW – TELL'.

You should break the whole demonstration down into a series of separate operations, using the 'Tell – Show – Tell' technique several times in several ways. Start to finish, it might go like this.

You sit down with your prospective customers and you tell them what you propose to show them. You tell them at the start all the things you propose to show them.

Then you proceed with the demonstration, taking each separate operation and using 'Tell – Show – Tell' again, this time reminding the customers of what you told them you would show them, then showing them, with no talking, then telling them again what they've just seen and asking if they're happy with that or would they like to see it again. (You'll need to read this paragraph slowly at least three times, just as if you were attending a demonstration!)

When you've completed all the 'Tell – Show – Tell' separate operations, you recap on everything the customers have seen, telling them everything once again, then you ask if they have any questions or if they would like to go through the entire demonstration again, from start to finish, or any specific part of the demonstration.

If you are demonstrating something which *must* go from start to finish non-stop, so that it's not possible to break it down into separate operations, then demonstrate the entire process at least twice, preferably three times, using the 'Tell – Show – Tell' technique each time.

I know this all sounds far too much trouble, even patronising for the customer. I just know it's the best way, the most thorough way, to conduct a demonstration, that's all. It's the winner's way.

Closing Time!

All doubts resolved: all 'Tell – Show – Tells' completed; you can now provide the customers with whatever literature is relevant to what you've just done and you can close in exactly the same way you would have done if you'd been going through a Proposal with them.

'You're happy with everything? Can we go ahead then?'

Now let's look at some specific techniques and attitudes which can help and hinder during a demonstration.

Getting the customer involved

It's always good to get the customers involved – to let them try it for themselves. But only if you are confident that the customers will be able to do it right first time. If you have any kind of situation where there is a knack required, or training and experience required to master a procedure or function, *don't let the customers anywhere near it.*

Whatever you say, if they muff it they'll go away thinking it's going to be too complicated or too difficult for their staff to handle. Their ego will lose you the order.

I'll never forget a visit many years ago to an old-fashioned toffee factory. During the tour of the factory, our party passed through a quaint little room, completely bare except for several wooden stakes sticking a foot out of the walls, about head high. This ancient chap in a brown smock was kneading a hefty chunk of semi-molten toffee. He'd manipulate the toffee with incredibly smooth, flowing motions, turning it from a round ball into a sausage shape and then, with a kind of flick of his wrists, he'd throw the sausage up over a wooden stake, catch the two ends as they slowly flowed downwards and knead the two halves into a ball again. Guess you should have been there!

Our guide asked if any of the party would like to have a go. It was an obvious set up, but we all tried. And every time, all we got were two lumps of molten toffee on the floor. None of us could master the wooden stake bit. Half of our party couldn't even throw the toffee high enough to reach the stake. Everyone had a good laugh. Our guide explained that old George, the guy in the brown smock, had been doing this for 40 years, and was the only employee who could knead toffee properly. 'Don't know what we're going to do when he retires. He's 68 now. He learned his trade from his father, but his daughter doesn't want to know. Quality's bound to suffer when we have to knead with these new-fangled machines!'

You're not likely to suffer from any 'knack traps' like this one, but the message is clear.

Respect your product

Don't bang it, slap it, kick it, toss it, lean on it or abuse it in any way whatsoever. Caress it, drool over it, revere it. It's the best product in the whole world and that's what the customer has to go away thinking.

Your superiority depends entirely on the respect you show your product. Remember the two directors who went shopping for filing cabinets?

Don't be an exhibitionist

Things *will* go wrong from time to time. Murphy's law strikes anywhere, in spite of the best-laid plans and preparations. When they do, play it down. Often the customers won't even be aware that something's gone wrong unless you tell them.

A classic example of this occurred several years ago in Birmingham. A regional manager and one of his salesmen were demonstrating a small offset printing machine to two prospective customers. Halfway through the demonstration, a panel in the side of the machine came undone. The manager saw the panel beginning to fall away and, with the flat of his hand, pushed it back into place. The customers were on the other side of the machine, watching it perform, and saw nothing of the problem. But the manager caught the palm of his hand on the edge of the panel, and gashed his hand pretty dreadfully – about a five-centimetre cut.

Now most salespeople in that predicament would instantly become martyrs, holding their blood dripping hand high and screaming, 'Oh my God!' The customers would thereupon be convinced that they'd been looking at a highly dangerous piece of equipment, and wouldn't buy it at any price.

This particular manager was a professional. His bleeding hand went instantly into his trouser pocket and he kept going with the demonstration as if nothing had happened. Five minutes later he could feel the blood trickling into his shoe, so he passed the demonstration to his salesman and excused himself, pleading that nature called.

A few minutes later, his secretary goes up to the salesman to apologise on behalf of the manager that he's been called home urgently as one of his children had fallen and broken a leg, and his wife needed help. Sympathetic understanding from the customers. The demonstration was concluded. The order was won.

Privacy and thanks

Two golden rules for demonstrations which are conducted at other customers' premises.

Allow the prospective customers and your existing customers to talk privately together out of your earshot. If you hover, and are seen to be hovering, the prospective customers will get the idea you don't want them to talk privately to your customer, and they'll wonder why. Much better if you say to both of them, 'I'm sure you two would like to discuss things without me being around, so that you can get a really impartial picture of what our products can do. I'll just pop over to the toilets and be back in 10 minutes, okay?'

Second golden rule – make a point of thanking everyone concerned. It's so easy, in the heat and pressure of the moment, to forget to do this, and it's critical if you want to use this customer again for a future demonstration. Be appreciative and they'll appreciate you and be happy to help. Be appreciative in front of your prospective customers. They'll see for themselves the pleasure your thanks gives those people. They'll see for themselves how they want to help you. Your esteem as a professional goes up a few points in everyone's eyes.

F.A.B.

When you're going through the 'Tell – Show – Tell' routine, don't forget to use:

F.A.B.
Feature – Advantage – Benefit.

It's incredibly easy during a demonstration to talk about, point out, show, *features* of the product, and forget to explain the advantages and benefits that the customer gets from those features. Set out next are some examples of the way it *should* be done.

'You'll see that this machine has very large main bearings (feature) which means that you can take much deeper cuts than normal (advantage) and so your total machining time is drastically reduced (benefit)'.

'The casting we use is minimum centimetre-thick spheroidal graphite cast iron (feature) which means that even when the machine is not grouted into your factory floor there is absolutely no vibration (advantage), and that means you can expect a quality of surface finish which will cut out a lot of your grinding operations (benefit).'

Across-the-desk demonstrations

Many products can be effectively demonstrated to a prospective customer across his desk. Even products too large for this can be miniaturised for use in the hands of the competent professional salesperson.

The range and the scope are enormous. The ordinary central heating water valve to the high pressure corrosive chemicals process plant butterfly valve, all can be part cut-away to show the actual workings of the valve, so that a salesperson can demonstrate everything that needs to be demonstrated, across a desk.

Six different sizes of specially cut-away, nicely finished samples in the boot of the car, and the salesperson can tailor the demonstration precisely to the size of valves this particular customer or that particular customer uses.

One British valve manufacturer produces what is called a Security valve – a gate valve or ball valve fitted with a special rod that slides through holes in the hand wheel and into a hole in the valve body. Once the valve is set to the required position for use, the rod is padlocked into place so that only the key holder can adjust the flow through the pipes that the valve controls.

The salesperson might walk into a prospective customer's office with the security valve in his hand and ask: 'Do you get any problems in your process pipelines with vandals, or kids, or your own people changing the valve positions?'

It's a cert that he does. Jam factories, breweries, oil depots, even the central-heating system in a large office complex. As winter approaches, people don't put on sweaters; they turn the heating up. It costs thousands.

'What have you done about stopping these problems occurring?'

'Have you considered using valves like these?' The salesperson hands over his security valve sample and proceeds to give an across-the-desk demonstration.

I haven't got an obsession about valves, it's just they're so easy for everyone to identify with. One sales engineer I know sells a particularly fine valve for corrosive chemicals that will seal absolutely 100% at pressures of 2000 pounds per square inch. He uses a cut-away sample to demonstrate the internal construction of his valve, its neoprene rubber seating and its superbly moulded ptfe butterfly. But he can't demonstrate to prove that it won't leak at 2000 psi.

So he compromises, and adds a bit of fun. 'I can't prove to you that this valve seals absolutely 100% at 2000 psi, Mr Jones, but I can prove to you that it does at room pressure. If you promise to be very careful – this is one of my best suits – pour some of your scalding hot coffee into this valve and I'll sit here for as long as you think is reasonable with it directly over private parts just to show you it won't drip.'

'Nine out of ten customers say, "I believe you!" and laugh', the sales engineer claims. 'But every now and again you get one awkward so-and-so with a shaky hand...!'

Like the regional manager with the cut hand, I bet he puts the cleaning bills on his expenses as 'fair wear and tear in the line of duty'.

Demonstrating at exhibitions

Whatever the exhibition, whatever the product, if a demonstration is being conducted on a trade exhibition stand, there's always a crowd of people around that stand. Nothing attracts casual prospects as effectively as the demonstration. That combination of noise and movement – and curiosity.

Demonstrations at exhibitions involve continuous preparation, demonstrating, clearing up, preparation, demonstration, clearing up, preparation – and so on. All day, all week. Exhausting work, but highly productive work.

I've seen stands selling rotary concrete floor levellers, a bit like rotary lawn mowers but with flat paddles like old Indian ceiling fans, where a gang of labourers were mixing and shovelling concrete all day so that the demonstration could run. They filled a skip with the debris every day of the exhibition.

I've seen a true entrepreneurial salesman crack a big problem for his company's product with a pretty way-out, but highly effective demonstration at an agricultural show. You won't believe the name of the product – its called Bloat Guard!

The story goes like this. When cows eat fresh, dewy, green grass, they tend to make pigs of themselves. The fresh green grass effervesces in the cow's stomach and the cow gets very bloated. This affects the quality and quantity of the milk produced. One teaspoonful of Bloat Guard in the cow's drinking water twice a day and this problem is completely resolved.

Bloat Guard comes in bottles, so the agricultural show stand looked a lot like an old American West's medicine man's stall. And the farmers weren't having any! Farmers are by nature a very cynical lot.

This one salesman created queues, clamouring to buy Bloat Guard, with a very simple demonstration. He acquired a large clear PVC bag and a crate of Guinness. His assistant stood ready with a bottle of Bloat Guard and a spoon.

Barker fashion, he gathered a group of farmers around him.

'Imagine this plastic bag is your cow's stomach' he told his audience. 'When the cow eats too much fresh dewy green grass, the inside of the stomach looks like this...'. And he took an opened bottle of Guinness, put his thumb over the open top, shook the bottle violently for ten seconds and emptied its entire contents into the plastic bag, holding the bag in his fist, like a balloon about to be blown up. The Guinness, escaping into the larger area of the bag after being violently roused, frothed madly, filling the bag with brown foaming bubbles.

'And this is what Bloat Guard does' – the salesman's assistant adds one teaspoonful of Bloat Guard to the foaming mass of Guinness and, immediately, all the froth is gone and a flat calm is seen on the lake of Guinness in the bag. Incredibly effective. The speed of the transformation takes everyone completely by surprise.

What we don't know is whether those farmers who queued for a bottle intended to apply it to their cows, or to a bottle of Guinness down at the pub on Sunday! But does it matter? The word is spreading about Bloat Guard.

A braver man than I

In 1977, I returned home from the USA with 50 per cent of the patent on a portable 'hang it on your belt, camper's water purifier. Two aluminium containers, one for the dirty stream water, one for the purified, drinkable water, and a plastic gubbins, which contained the secret ingredient X. It all went into a neat little zip-up plastic case.

A few months later I came upon this brave chap from the Middle East, who went into raptures when he saw my water purifier and started chanting, 'We'll sell a million, we'll sell a million!'

'To whom?' I asked.

'The armies out there in the desert. They keep poisoning the wells, you know. The soldiers are falling like flies. Will it filter out metallic poisons? If it will, or sufficiently to get the chap to hospital before his toes turn up, we'll sell a million of 'em – maybe two million.'

I took a couple of sample water purifiers to a chemical analyst and asked him to test the unit's effectiveness with metallic poisons. The analyst didn't work up any enthusiasm for the job. Guess a million purifiers to the Middle East and a Queen's Award for Export didn't feature in his world. No sense of humour, either.

Three weeks later, I had the analyst's report. Yes. No problems with metallic poisons. I cabled my man in the Middle East.

Two weeks later, I received a telephone call from this very excitable individual. 'Sell five million!' he kept saying.

'Find out if it'll cope with what?' I had a bit of a problem grasping the significance of his latest request for an analyst's report. 'The man's mad,' I thought.

But I went back to my chemical analyst, conveyed our latest request and, impressing upon him the urgency of the matter, waited for the results of the tests. It took him two hours. When he reported back there wasn't a glimmer of a smile on his face, not a twitch, as he said, 'Perfectly safe – but it will taste rather salty'.

He didn't even smile when I nearly fell off his chair with laughing so much.

Another cable to my man in the Middle East and I sat back to await results. A month later he was in my office, gleefully relating what had happened at his demonstration.

'It took me weeks to get all six of the Sheikhs together,' he told me. 'I wanted to do this once only! At last I had 'em all lined up for the demonstration. Three interpreters going nineteen to the dozen, and twenty or more bodyguards on all sides. I went through the construction of the unit, its potential uses for their armies, the expected life of the active ingredients. I told them about our analyst's report on the metallic poisons – gave them each a copy.

'Then I took a deep breath, unzipped my fly, peed into the thing, filtered it, and drank it all down in one go.

'And do you know what those Sheikhs did? They got down on their knees and they kissed the ground in front of me like I was Allah himself!'

I poured him a stiff drink. I only wish I could have been out there on the day of the demonstration to pour him one then. A braver man than I, that's for sure.

Conducted tours of the works

No way can your supremacy be better demonstrated than with a conducted tour of your works. Or the opposite: meaning your incompetence!

In the middle of the tour of the works might well be the demonstration, but we've adequately covered that bit. This final piece in this chapter is concerned with those aspects of the customer's visit to your place of business not directly involved with the demonstration itself.

Let's picture the *perfect* tour of the works, with a few alternatives to perfection thrown in.

The chairman's chauffeur picks up the prospective customer in the chairman's Rolls. It usually stands outside the front offices most of the day, if the chairman's in, just taking up space. It's an asset that costs the company a lot of money. So use it as an asset. Requisition it to bring this very important prospective customer to your place of business.

Second best: *you* collect the customer in your car. But your car has been specially prepared for the task. All the junk has been removed. All the literature is safely stowed away in the boot, along with the kiddy seat that usually hangs on the back seat. Interior is freshly vacuumed. Exterior freshly washed and leathered. No smoking inside the car until you're sure the customer does. No pop music, or any kind of music on the cassette player. And drive carefully, allowing plenty of time.

Welcome to UWC

Another second best; the customer drives to your place of business in his own car, and when he arrives, *he's expected.* When he stops at the main gate, the security man says – 'Ah yes sir, Mr Jones sir. Welcome to UWC. If you drive over there to the main entrance, you'll find a parking place just to the left of the main doors. Your name will be on it. It's our chairman's spot, but he's not in.'

And sure enough, there's a little notice hanging on the chairman's name stake saying 'Reserved for Mr Jones, Apex Distributors Ltd' today.'

When Mr Jones walks into your main reception, the first thing he sees is your notice 'UWC welcomes Mr Jones of Apex Distributors Ltd'. And, even better, everything has been spelt correctly. Your receptionist has been warned by the security man that Mr Jones is on his way in, and has telephoned you and your chief. She gets up as Mr Jones enters, walks towards him smiling, hand extended, and says, 'Mr Jones. Good morning. Welcome to UWC. Mr Fenton and Mr

Carstairs are on their way down. Would you like to visit the men's room before they get here? Let me look after your coat.'

'Customers on the Premises' mode

More than that. As soon as the customer drives past the main gate, the security man presses the 'Customer on the Premises' button, bells ring in every department and *everyone* changes into 'being happy and bustle' mode. Everywhere is a happy, throbbing hive of positive activity whilst the customer is around. Any dismal Jimmies get fired for sabotage!

The conducted tour of the works gets under way. It's planned like a royal procession, with drawings and route markers. And everyone on the route knows it's coming their way, and what to do and not to do. UWC is the kind of company in which everyone understands that it's the customers that pay their wages every week or every month.

The departments covered by the tour fall into MUSTS, SHOULDS and COULDS categories.

MUSTS include the **purchasing department.** 'We think you should see how our purchasing people make sure our lines of supply are always kept secure, with at least two sources of supply active for every bought-in component and sub-assembly. This is important to you because it plays a key part in our policy never to let any customer down on delivery.' Don't forget to show him the 'UWC instructions to suppliers' procedure in action.

Goods inwards inspection. 'These are the people who make sure that the bought-out items ordered by our purchasing people come in undamaged and at the right quality. George Goodwin here and his two assistants have a system for checking and chasing that they claim is absolutely infallible. I'll let George tell you about that.'

Goods outwards inspection and despatch. 'This is our last line of inspection before the product reaches the customer. Every single unit is thoroughly inspected and then packed for despatch, by the same staff. Any doubts whatsoever, and the unit goes back to final production inspection with a red "TOP PRIORITY" notice on it, because any delay from then on could mean we risk breaking our delivery promise.'

Finished goods stores. 'You'll see from just looking at all this how many of our products we keep in stock for immediate delivery. We aim never to fall below 90% of the total range at any one time, with 100% for anything that falls into the 80/20 law. You know, 20 per cent of our products are used by 80 per cent of our customers. That 20% we've *always* got in stock.'

Quality control. 'This is the quality control and final inspection department for everything we manufacture ourselves. You'll see we use the most up-to-date technology throughout. All Covered by ISO 9000, of course. Coupled with our range of numerical controlled machines in production itself, this makes us a clear number one in our industry for quality, reliability and longest working life. Our Research and Development people are also number one, which is why we are so far ahead of our competitors. We can't show you R & D, I'm afraid. There's a fair bit going on in there for the Ministry of Defence and it's a classified area.'

Production and assembly. 'Let's start at the beginning and follow the manufacturing and assembly process through. Then you'll see our widget crusher taking shape as we go and when we get to the end you'll be able to test one yourself as it comes off final assembly.'

The sales department. 'I'm sure you'd like to meet the people who will be looking after your orders. I know they'd like to meet you. Putting a face to a voice on the telephone is very important, don't you think? This is Harry Chandley. He looks after our sales estimating. This is Gloria Prufrock. She sees that any telephone requests for information are dealt with speedily. As you can see, she's in communication with stores and other departments by VDU as well as by phone and personal bleeper. If the person with the answer is sitting on the loo, we can still reach him or her inside 10 seconds.'

After-sales service. 'You'll see here how we can get a service engineer to you within four hours, if one of your people backs a forklift truck into a unit or something. All twenty-seven of our service engineers drive a fully equipped van and are in constant communication with base. They have mobile phones, so that if they're away from their van, on a job, we can still get in touch with them and they with us.'

Customer training school. 'This is where your own people will come for their three-day course on how to get the very best out of their widget crushers. This is optional and all part of the service we give our customers. About 85 per cent take us up on the training course. It means our products are earning money for our customers a good deal sooner, and a bit faster every day thereafter.'

Beware the junk room. Every conducted tour I've been on – and that's a lot – has had a classic Achilles heel; the part of the works no one thinks about, so no one allows for. The junk room!

It may not be a junk room; it may be the department or bay of the factory that's being redecorated, redeployed, re-organised or made redundant. Doesn't matter. To the customer it looks like a junk room, and it kills the conducted tour of the works stone dead.

Every conducted tour I've been on has passed right through the middle of the junk room. No one's thought of the significance. No one's planned, therefore, to avoid it.

You *must* avoid it at all costs, even to the extent of postponing the tour until the junk is cleared up, or, if the junk room is permanent and in a critically strategic place, until it's been moved to a rented garage about three miles away from the factory.

Chances are, as you read this, you don't even know where your junk room is, or how many of them you've got. Get out there and find out. Act like a professional golfer – walk the course before the match.

The boardroom lunch

The highlight of any conducted tour of the works is when the visiting customer is given lunch in the boardroom, and all the directors present (and that means all the directors, properly briefed) ply the customer with questions about his business and how he sees business in general. He walks out of that boardroom after lunch, ten feet tall. He'll buy from you for life. No one's ever before made him feel so important.

Hopefully, if you're the salesperson looking after that customer, you get invited to that boardroom lunch, too. Nothing is more degrading than to be left out of the lunch, on the grounds that your salary scale is four and only executives at seven or above are allowed into the boardroom. Nothing is more certain to make the customer himself very aware that the person who looks after his account is of minor importance in his future supplier's hierarchy.

I've seen salespeople who have been taking a customer round the works excluded from lunch in the senior staff canteen, let alone the boardroom. Sheer stupidity. Internal politics getting in the way of business, again. If you can't get this stupidity changed, then ALWAYS use an outside quality restaurant.

The farewells

The final crucial point to get right on a successful conducted tour of the works is the goodbye. It's essential that the most senior executive who has been involved in the tour, or part of the tour, walks all the way to the customer's car with him, opens the car door, shakes him by the hand, and stands and waves him goodbye as he drives away.

The security man has been phoned. The barrier is up and he too waves goodbye as the customer drives past.

Bells ring the all clear. Customer's *off* the premises. Phew! Now we can all get back to work. 'Harry! What the bloody 'ell went wrong with that meeting this morning? Never seen such a militant lot of morons. Can't you keep your people working for even one hour a day? And George, the mess we had to clear up in bay three before that customer came through. You'll do it yourself next time!'

You don't have to be big

You don't have to be a big company to organise a successful conducted tour of the works. You should get used to doing them as often as you can, because, apart from their value as business generators, there's nothing remotely comparable as a reason for keeping the entire operation neat and tidy, and all the people on their toes. And that means *more efficient.*

90 per cent of all the business that is quoted for throughout industry and commerce is lost because the Quotation doesn't do the job it is supposed to do.

The traditional Quotation is the most stupid document in business – only suppliers who are the cheapest price and the shortest delivery can win with it. The rest must change – or eventually die.

We certainly don't want to be the cheapest – so our options are clear.

Chapter 3

How to Present Your Proposals

Let's get the definitions right before we get started.

A **quotation,** the traditional document used by most of industry and commerce the world over to confirm in writing what is being offered for sale, is *a legal document*. It contains just about every reason why the prospective customer *should not* place the order with you...

Specification or list of items being offered
(meaningless: doesn't have any 'what's in it for the customer!')

Price (How much???)

Delivery (Too long!)

Terms of Payment (Too short!)

E & 0 E (That little term at the bottom of the page that means 'Errors and Omissions Excepted' – a rough translation could be 'Whatever we've said we don't really mean!')

Victoriana (Phrases like 'Thank you for your esteemed enquiry' and 'We look forward to the favour of your valued order which will receive our most careful attention', which make modern customers think this particular supplier is still living in the days of the first Industrial Revolution).

Your Terms and Conditions (All that pale grey or blue small print on the back. Why now? Why this early, before the customer's agreed to buy? Wouldn't on the back of your acknowledgement of the order be more appropriate?)

Price only holds good for 30 days (Then the customer has to start all over again? Did anyone consider how long it takes for the average customer to get through his decision-making process?)

You know, businesses which aren't trading at lowest price and shortest delivery and which are using these kind of legal 'Quotation' documents really are still thinking as if they were in the first Industrial Revolution. That was the first big time when Demand outstripped Supply by several hundred miles. So suppliers could dictate terms.

Now it's the other way round. Customers dictate terms and suppliers jump or lose the customers. At least that's the way the customers see it – and they've a pretty good edge – it's their money that pays our wages!

This book is about us salespeople getting that edge back again. But *not* by changing the Supply and Demand cycle round again. As I said earlier, we're going to do it by positive, aggressive professional *Selling.*

Quotations are *out.* Proposals are in.

So let's define what I mean by the word **Proposal.**

A **Proposal** is a Selling tool. A Quotation is not.

A Proposal contains all the reasons why the prospective customer *should* place the order with you. It is an invaluable selling aid, especially if your price is higher than your competitors'. Used correctly, it greatly increases the odds in your favour.

Format for the Best Proposal

The best Proposals are designed with five sections. These sections must be used in the proper order. They are these:

1 The Customer's Objectives

The Proposal should begin by re-stating the objectives that the customer wishes to achieve. These will have been established during previous sales meetings, recorded carefully (see Chapter 4), and should be listed in priority order – the most important first. Thus, when the prospective customer picks up the Proposal and begins to read it, the first thing he reads after his name, address and introductory paragraph is what he and his business wants to achieve. Whatever he may have been wrapped up in before he began reading, this 'Objectives' first section is guaranteed to make him switch his concentration to the project for which you are presenting the Proposal. So he's in the right frame of mind before he gets into the meat of the matter.

2 Your Recommendations

Having defined the customer's objectives, you then present a condensed picture of the goods or services you are recommending that will achieve these objectives, together with brief outlines of how each objective will be achieved, using the same priority order. For complicated equipment, specification sheets can be added to the Proposal (at the back) and referred to in this section.

3 Summary of Additional Benefits

The principal benefits that this particular customer will derive from what you are proposing to sell him will undoubtedly have been mentioned in Section 2. If there are any additional benefits which this customer will enjoy, other than those already mentioned, and providing they are relevant to this particular customer, they should be listed.

When you list them, make sure they are benefits, not features.

4 Financial Justification

This is the most important section. Very few people buy anything unless they can see clearly that the goods or services they are considering will show them an adequate profit; or saving, which ultimately comes to the same thing. They also look for that adequate profit happening in as short a time as they can achieve – the 'pay back' period or amortization of the purchase price.

The majority of salespeople expect their customers to work all this out for themselves. Some of them do. Many of them don't. One thing I know for sure – a salesperson who works it all out for the customer, and presents the financial justification in the Proposal, always has a very appreciative customer and is always top in confidence and knowledge when the time comes to close the sale. So these kinds of salespeople usually win hands down.

Financial justification can be written into a Proposal in many different ways, as you will see from the examples later in this chapter. The rule on which way to use is very clear and simple. If the purchase can be financially justified in three different ways, you use all three ways, the best first, and you finish by adding the three lots of savings or gains together to produce a final amortization figure, or total profit/savings figure.

5   Your Guarantees and After-Sales Service

Don't leave the guarantee, warranty and after-sales service details to the pale grey small print on the back of the Quotation. It's much more important. In the mind of that prospective customer, it might be the most important factor of all. If anything goes wrong, he carries the can, not you. He could even get fired for making a stupid decision and buying what you're proposing. That's maybe not the reality, but it's how they think. So put their minds at rest. Tell the customers how good your guarantees and your service are. How fast your service engineers respond.

And back it all up with some third-party references. Customers who you know will be happy to take a call from one of your prospective customers and will sing your praises loud and clear – because you've asked them if they will do this, well in advance. Every really professional competition beater has at least a dozen such third party references tucked away, ready to use, at all times.

Such a five section Proposal can be constructed in the form of a letter, or as a series of separate sheets, one for each section, wrapped up in a professional-looking binder. Whichever format you use, the good old legal Quotation document can *still* be added – at the back, after the specification sheets – if your company's legal eagles insist that traditions must be maintained at all costs!

Making the change from Quotation to Proposal

Over the years, as a consultant, I've helped many businesses change over from the Quotation deterrent to the Selling Proposal.

A change of format, from quotation to proposal, can have startling effects on the Quotes to Order Ratio. In a single year, one of the companies that adopted this system improved from:

25 Quotes to 1 Order
to
4.5 Quotes to 1 Order

So working the numbers through, for the same number of Quotes (or rather Proposals now) submitted, they were winning more than FIVE TIMES AS MANY ORDERS.

Here are a few examples:

Example 1
The original quotation

GKN Sankey Limited
automatic vending division

J.B. & Company
Blagdon Road,
Swindon
Wilts

For the attention of A.J. Holt Esq.

Fully comprehensive rental over 5 years

3 x Model S32 SUPERMATIC Hot 'n Cold Drink Vending Machines

each   £60.95 per month + VAT

(total £182.85 per month + VAT)

Prices as quoted unless otherwise stated to include delivery to site and commissioning by a Service Engineer on a prepared site as specified in our installation data sheet.

Delivery time   7-10 days

Payment terms – Nett cash thirty days from invoice

This quotation is subject to the conditions stated here and printed on the back hereof and is open to acceptance within   30 days

FOR GKN SANKEY LIMITED

K.D.TAYLOR

Field Sales Manager

Example 1
The subsequent quotation

GKN Sankey Limited
automatic vending division

A J Holt Esq
J B & Company
Blagdon Road
Swindon
Wilts

Dear Mr. Holt,

Thank you for your help last Thursday and for the useful figures you supplied; the opportunity to carry out a survey of your plant was also much appreciated. From our conversation I understand your requirements are:-

- A drinks service for 325 shift workers plus 110 day workers and 28 staff.

- Availability of this service throughout the 24 hours three shift working with minimum attention, and accessibility for office staff during the day.

- A charge of 4p to be maintained for tea, but other drinks to be set initially at 5p. Provision for vend price increases to be built in.

- The additional facility of a chilled drink selection to alleviate the humid working conditions in the moulding shops.

- A Pepsi Cola or Coca-Cola selection as specifically requested by the female packers through their committee member.

- The total operation to be self-supporting.

Our recommendations

I believe your requirements will be adequately and economically covered by the provision on rental of 3 x Model S32 SUPERMATIC Hot 'n Cold drinks vending machines. One of these to be sited as shown at A on the enclosed layout plan of your plant. This is convenient to the packing and finishing section and is in a suitable location for the office staff. The remaining two machines to be sited as shown at B and C in the main and semi-automatic moulding machine shops.

All these locations are convenient for power and water supplies and give the best optimum sitings having regard to the proximity of the majority of the workforce.

Summary of Benefits

The SUPERMATIC Rental Package has the following benefits:

1 The machine provides 29 selections of hot tea, coffee, chocolate, and soup plus 3 selections of refrigerated chilled drinks. Two of the latter are carbonated, which means that fizzy drinks including Pepsi or Coca-Cola can be enjoyed by your packing girls.

2 The tea and coffee selections can be set to give a total of 29 variants to suit a wide range of personal preferences.

3 The unique Sankey coin handling system accepts lp, 2p and 5p coins, inserted in any order to totalise up to 29 pence. Therefore your price level requirements of 4p and 5p can be catered for. In fact three price levels can be utilised, and possible future increases, caused perhaps by commodity prices, are a matter of simple on-site adjustment.

4 The cup capacity of 550 drinks in each machine ensures that your entire labour force can be catered for over a 24-hour period with only one daily filling and cleaning operation.

5 The fixed monthly rental payments are inclusive of:

- free delivery to your prepared site
- comprehensive insurance cover
- commissioning and full instruction
- full maintenance including parts and labour
- an initial supply of cups and ingredients representing about 3500 drinks,

and are guaranteed inflation-proof for the entire period of the agreement.

6 These payments will be more than covered by the income generated by revenue from the machines.

Financial Consideration

The basis for operating figures are CUP COSTINGS including appropriate recommended ingredients and the cup itself. Average take-off figures are based on the findings of the Tavistock Institute of Human Relations, and statistics supplied by the Automatic Vending Association. They have been marginally adjusted to suit the special conditions existing in your plant.

Drink	Cost/cup	Average t/o	Vend price	Cup Profit	Profit per 100
Tea	1.57p	10%	4p	2.43p	24.03p
Coffee	2.67p	35%	5p	2.33p	81.55p
Choc	2.66p	15%	5p	2.34p	35.10p
Soup	1.72p	15%	5p	3.28p	49.20p
Cold	1.62p	25%	5p	3.38p	84.50p
	100				**274.65p**

Therefore average cup profit = 2.75 pence.

The monthly rental premium for each machine based on your current Regional Development Grant qualification is £60.95, which is equivalent to a daily cost of £ 3.04.

If we divide this figure by the average profit of 2.75p, we arrive at a daily requirement of 110 drinks per 24 hours per machine to break even. At this point, rental charges and ingredients costs have been covered.

If only 80% of your total workforce took a very conservative 2 drinks per day, this would account for an average daily off-take of 246 drinks per machine:

463	x 80%	=	370
370	x 2 drinks	=	740
740	÷ 3 M/cs.	=	246 per machine

In these circumstances, your break-even situation would be comfortably reached and you could look forward to a daily profit of £11.22.

246 – 110	=	136.
136 x 2.75	=	374p.
374 x 3 M/cs.	=	£11.22.

If we allow the odd £1.22 for daily cleaning labour cost, the total profit over the 5-year period would be £12,000 (£10 x 20 Days x 60 Months).

To this must be added the present cost in labour and materials of your existing tea service. Your personnel manager's figures were £1,250 last year, of which £1,020 was wages. Allowing for the projected rate of inflation in labour costs over the next five years, we arrive at a figure of £8,827 and this amount represents the additional saving which will be made.

Over the five years therefore we have:

vending profit		£12,000
plus:	cost savings	£8,627

TOTAL		£20,827

I would like to confirm that any service requirement will be cheerfully and promptly attended to by our locally-based engineer, Charlie Newman, who is fully trained and adequately equipped. As part of the Rental package this service would be without charge.

I have enclosed a cup costing chart for your interest and in support of the financial calculations; also a technical data leaflet which includes installation requirements.

Finally, I have included a Rental Agreement and would be grateful if this could be completed as indicated and signed by yourself as the authorised signatory.

Yours sincerely,

Field Sales Manager.

Enc.:

    Quotation
    Cup Costing Chart
    Site Plan
    Installation Data
    Rental Agreement

Example 2

Our second example is for the replacement of a dishwasher in a large school kitchen – a very cost-conscious market and a supplier that competes with 400 (yes, four hundred) other suppliers and invariably finds itself higher on price. But its back-up is second to none.

The original quotation

Please reply to
The Hobart Manufacturing Company Limited
11 Railton Road, Kempston
Bedford MK42 7PW
Tel: 01234 841220 Fax: 01234 841219

[Customer name and
address withheld for
reasons of confidentiality]

Dear Madam,

RE: REPLACEMENT OF EXISTING DISHWASHER

Further to your most recent conversation with our Sales Executive, Stan Tyler, we are now pleased to submit the attached quotation together with running cost summary for the above.

You present Hobart dishwasher has a maximum throughput of 220 racks per hour. However, our calculations based upon approximately 450 lunches, 130 breakfasts, and 180 evening meals suggests that a machine with a 150 rack per hour throughput will be more appropriate and result in a considerable reduction in running costs.

Our recommendation is therefore, to incorporate a Hobart CXLA 150 Rack Conveyor Dishwasher; this machine features a Pre-wash Section, Powerful Main Wash Section and Hobart Dual Rinse System, and the modern technology incorporated into this machine not only ensures excellent results, easy operation, and supervision, but also provides exceptional economy in the use of power, water and detergents. To further enhance this economy, we have specified a Hobart C5 Heat Exchange Condenser Unit which recovers waste heat from the machine exhaust to pre heat incoming cold water.

Our proposal is to incorporate the new machine within your existing tabling layout. This will require some minor modification to the tabling which will automatically shut down the rinse systems and conveyor when the tabling is full. In addition, your existing ventilation ductwork will need modification to suit the CXLA and a budget sum is included.

Finally, we have included for full installation of the foregoing equipment including disconnection, removal, and laying aside of your existing machine by Hobart Technicians. All of the equipment specified carries a twelve-month parts and labour guarantee which automatically provides you with *Seven days per week breakdown cover at no extra cost*. Full staff training would be provided by either myself or Stan Tyler.

We do hope these details meet with your approval and look forward to discussing them further with you.

Yours sincerely

TIM BENDER
Technical Sales Executive

Example 2
The subsequent proposal

By Appointment to H M The Queen
Manufacturers of Kitchen Equipment
Hobart Manufacturing Company Limited
Trading as Hobart Still, London

Please reply to
The Hobart Manufacturing Company Limited
11 Railton Road, Kempston
Bedford MK42 7PW
Tel: 01234 841220 Fax: 01234 841219

Dear Madam,

RE: REPLACEMENT OF EXISTING DISHWASHER

Further to your most recent conversation with our Sales Executive, Stan Tyler, we are now pleased to submit details of a Hobart Warewashing Machine to suit your requirements.

Your Objectives

As we understand it, you are seeking to:

- replace your Hobart CC183 dishwasher with a modern machine of more appropriate capacity

- reduce the maintenance and operating costs of the dishwashing equipment

- improve 'dirties' handling but to retain existing ancillary equipment where possible.

Our Recommendations

Having discussed your requirements in detail with Stan Tyler, we recommend our model CXLA Rack Conveyor Dishwasher. The CXLA has a rack capacity of 150 racks per hour which will comfortably meet the warewashing requirements resulting from 450 lunches, 130 breakfasts and 180 evening meals. Furthermore, the CXLA includes an integral pre-wash section (not present in the existing machine) to ensure consistently excellent results. The Hobart CX Dual Rinse System will provide exceptional economies in your running costs.

We are also recommending a new section of 'dirties' tabling which will provide a handling system enabling your staff to operate more efficiently in loading the machine.

Additionally, a table-end switch fitted to the existing 'cleans' section will automatically shut down the rinse system and conveyor when the tabling is full.

The CXLA and complementary equipment represent real value for money and provide the most cost effective solution to the proposed upgrading of your warewashing facilities.

Summary of Additional Benefits of the Proposed Hobart CXLA Warewashing Machine

Side Mounted Wash Pumps

Powerful stainless steel wash pumps are mounted on the side of deep 'L-shaped' tanks. The results are constant wash performance; limited heat loss from the tank surface and complete draining of the pump when tanks are emptied. This reduction in bacterial growth conditions helps to maintain hygiene standards.

Strainer System

A two-part sloping strainer system and indented, anti-clog jets formed in stainless steel wash arms combine to prevent the break up and free distribution of food soil. Thus, detergent exhaustion and consumption are reduced whilst maintaining wash water conditions necessary for the best wash performance.

Dual Rinse System

The dual-rinse system delivers a high volume pre-final rinse combined with a sanitising fresh water final rinse with a relatively low water consumption. Energy consumption is correspondingly low and may be further reduced by means of an optional energy recovery condenser. Running costs are thereby less than with conventional rinse systems.

Machine filling

The CX 'Get Ready Button' controls the tank filling and heating whilst the drain interlocks provide heater protection and ensure drain closure when doors are closed. Digital display of temperatures and motor warning lights are prominently positioned on the central control panel. Operator attention required during machine filling and washing is kept to a minimum.

Tray sorting

The tray sorting system is based on the simple principle of 'a place for everything and everything in its place'. This gives an easy to follow procedure which maximised the capacity of the dishwasher. Consequently the machine need not be oversized to compensate for inefficient sorting and loading.

Reference Site

A machine similar to that proposed is in operation at Haberdasher's Askes School. Arrangements to view the machine can be made with Stan Tyler.

Your Investment

The existing dishwasher is oversized for present numbers and is not therefore being operated at optimum efficiency. Its replacement with the Hobart CXLA would result in savings in water, heating, detergent and rise aid costs. Conservatively we estimate these savings to be in the region of £2,500 per annum (see Schedule: Summary of Annual Operating Costs for details).

A mechanical pre-wash removes food particles which might otherwise enter the detergent-charged wash tank. Thus detergent solution rates (and costs) may be kept to a minimum. This could produce further savings of approximately £400.00 per annum.

Production of the CC183 ceased in 1986 and will be classified as 'obsolete' next year when normally replaceable spare parts will no longer be produced. Availability of such parts for current Hobart machines is assured for at least 10 years, providing peace for mind for continued satisfactory operation in years to come.

During the first year the CXLA would be under warranty which automatically provides you with seven days per week breakdown cover at not extra cost.

SUMMARY OF ANNUAL OPERATING COSTS

ALDENHAM SCHOOL		EXISTING HOBART CC-183 DISHWASHER	PROPOSED HOBART CXLA DISHWASHER WITH C5
ENERGY	MACHINE ENERGY REQUIREMENT (KW/HR)	64 kW	33 kW
	EXT ENERGY REQUIREMENT TO PRE-HEAT RINSE SUPPLY FROM 10° TO 50 °C	Nil	Nil
	TOTAL ENERGY USAGE PER 3 HR DAY	192 kW	99 kW
	COST PER DAY AT 7p PER KW/HR	£13.44	£6.93
	COST PER ANNUM (38 WEEKS) (7 DAYS PER WEEK)	£3,575.00	£1,843.00
WASTE	RINSE WATER CONSUMPTION LTRS/HR	660 litres (0.66m^3)	300 litres (0.3m^3)
	TOTAL WATER CONSUMPTION PER 3 DAY INCLUDING TANK FILLS PER DAY	2180 litres (2.18m^3)	1085 litres (1.08m^3)
	COST PER DAY (£1.00p/m^2)	£2.18	£1.08
	COST PER ANNUM (38 WEEKS) (7 DAYS PER WEEK)	£580.00	£288.00
CHEMICALS	APPROXIMATE DETERGENT COST (25 LITRES DRUM @ £50/DRUM)	£850.00 (17 drums)	£450.00 (9 drums)
	APPROXIMATE RINSE AID COST (25 LITRE DRUM @ £90/DRUM)	£900.00 (10 drums)	£450.00 (5 drums)
	TOTAL ANNUAL OPERATING COST	£5,905.00	£3,031.00
	TOTAL ANNUAL SAVING		£2,874.00

Discounts

I am pleased to be able to offer a substantial 20% discount on the list price for the recommended equipment, providing an all-in price of £23,227.40, as detailed below:

FINANCIAL SUMMARY

ITEM	DESCRIPTION	LIST PRICE £	DISCOUNT %	NETT PRICE £
1	Hobart CXLA Dishwasher	17,549.00	20	14,039.20
1a	C5 Energy Recovery Condenser	3,377.00	20	2,701.60
1b	Auto Timer (option)	509.00	20	407.20
1c	Insulated Panels (option)	2,153.00	20	1,722.40
2	Supply Table End Switch	152.00	Nett	152.00
3	New 'Dirties' Tabling (option)	1,655.00	Nett	1,655.00
	Sub-total Supply Only Basic Equipment	21,078.00		16,892.80
	Additional Cost for Options	4,317,00		3,784.60
	Modify Tabling and Fit Switch			200.00
	Installation			1.350.00
	Modify Ductwork (Provisional Sum)			1,000.00
	Grand Total: Fully Inclusive Nett			23,227.40

ALL PRICES EXCLUDE VAT

Finance Options

Hobart Equipment Leasing Limited can offer a range of finance products including Lease Rental, Full Warranty Lease and Lease Purchase. All are finance leases available over either three or five years.

Leasing is an inexpensive and tax efficient method of obtaining the use of new equipment. A Full Warranty Lease incorporates total service including parts and labour for the duration of the contract.

The Leasing Company

Hobart Equipment Leasing Limited (A member of the Consumer Credit Trade Association Licence No. 121213) is a wholly owned subsidiary of Hobart Still and has been trading for over ten years, providing a unique opportunity for the customer to obtain Hobart Still equipment, after sales service and finance from a 'single source'.

Leasing Illustration

For the supply and installation of all equipment including options and extras:-

3 Year Lease Rental:-
Advance Rental Payment (excl. VAT)   2,253.52
Followed by 11 Quarterly Rental
    Payments (excl. VAT)   2,253.52

OR

5 Year Full Warranty Lease:-
Advance Rental Payment (excl. VAT)   1,737.83,
Followed By 19 Quarterly Rental
    Payments (excl. VAT)   1,737.83

Service Support for your Hobart Still Equipment

We recognise the need to maintain and repair equipment during and after the guarantee period. A prompt effective response is required should any item fail to perform.

Hobart Still is committed to providing a quality service through experienced and well-trained technical Service Engineers.

All Hobart Still Technicians are trained in our own school at Peterborough where details of Technicians' individual training and skills are on record.

Our National Distribution Centre based at Peterborough holds £6.5 million of stock and overnight or even 'same day' delivery service is available.

Service will be provided from our London and Northern Home Counties Regional Office, details of which are listed below.

There are a number of Hobart Still Technicians within one hour of Aldenham School ensuring a quick response to any service call. Service cover all day, every day Monday to Friday. Contact the Regional Centre. Saturdays and Sundays dial 01345 830530, for the price of a local call.

Your Service Region

London & Home Counties Regional Office, The Hobart Mfg Co Ltd
11 Railton Road
Wosley Business Park, Kempston
Bedfordshire
MK42 7PW

Telephone:	01234 841220
No. of technicians & Supervisors:	90 & 9
Service Manager:	Jeff Luck
Technical Support Manager:	Colin Dowler
Customer Support Manager:	Terry Delaney
National Service Manager:	Jim Peden

Service

Emergency Call Out Service

• Guaranteed call out other than exceptional circumstances. Same day if call received before 10am., any others next working day.

• First time repair on 95% of total call outs including 3rd party equipment.

• National centralised spare parts holding is £6.5 million supporting individual Technician van stocks.

• Hobart Still provide emergency weekend cover at no premium charge.

We submit these proposals with the confidence that we can fully satisfy your requirements.

Stan Tyler will contact you shortly in order to finalise details and confirm your delivery expectations.

In the meantime, should you require any immediate assistance, please do not hesitate to contact me at the Regional Office, 01234 841220.

Yours faithfully,

TIM BENDER

Technical Sales Executive

Longer but not longer!

It must be obvious that doing the job of quoting properly gives you a much longer document. But it will not be much longer in terms of time to produce the document. Initially, you'll have a one-off set-up time to get all your standard paragraphs assembled on your Sales Office PC or your home lap top.

After that, the high speed number crunching capabilities of today's PC take over and you have your tailored proposal in two minutes with the minimum of keyboard typing.

And for the simpler supplier (job wise!) here is an example of a PC master format where only the Customer's Objectives and the Prices have to be customised. Everything goes on a page and a half of letter, plus a few pre-printed pages added to cover the PROOF section.

Template Proposal

CORPORATE CLOTHING FOR INDIVIDUALS   *EXECUTIVE IMAGE*

Executive Image Ltd. Unit 15 Castleton Close, Armley Road, Leeds LS12 2DS. Fax: (0532) 341966 Tel: (0532) 341977

Draft Proposal

Dear – -

Thank you for your enquiry. We present below our proposals for the supply of your new, corporate uniform.

Your Objectives

From our conversation we understand your requirements to be as follows:

1.
2.
3.

Our Recommendations

Our approach is very flexible, we do not issue a rigid style brochure but rather a portfolio of designs that can be manufactured in your choice of colour and fabric.

The enclosed styles and fabrics are (subject to confirmation) available for repeat orders with no minimums for at least 2 years. On request we can source additional fabrics and our design team can, without obligation, interpret your own ideas into sample garments.

In addition your company logo can be embroidered or printed onto any garments.

Measurement & Delivery

We have several options available for ensuring that your staff receive correctly fitting garments. The actual methods can be discussed with you to ascertain which is best for your company.

Delivery is usually 4-6 weeks from receipt of an order subject to fabric availability. Alternatively we have a 10-day express service. Full details can be sent on request. We will make every endeavour to meet any special date.

Your Investment

Our prices are based on a genuine commitment to a high quality standard together with offering the very best value for money.

Normal Delivery
Ladies Jacket	£xxx	+ VAT
Plain Skirt	£xxx	+ VAT
Pleated Skirt	£xxx	+ VAT
Blouse	£xxx	+ VAT

Extra for Express Delivery
Jacket	£10.00	+ VAT extra
Plain Skirt/Trouser	£5.00	+ VAT extra
Shirt/Blouse	£3.00	+ VAT extra

Reliability

The difference between ourselves and a mail order catalogue company is that we can visit you at your convenience to discuss your project in detail, propose solutions that are best for your company and avoid costly mistakes.

All garments are carefully inspected before despatch.

Enclosed is our client list together with vendor assessments from DHL International for the last 2 years.

We hope you decide to use our company as your corporate clothing supplier. We would value your business highly and prove that we are people who really care about our customers.

I will ring you in a few days.

Yours sincerely

You don't have to work out the figures every time

The next example shows the first two pages of a standard format used for proposals for high value capital equipment by Foundry & Technical Liaison Ltd of Willenhall, Staffs.

Even though I'm going to show you how to work out the figures later, you can devise one single representative example of the financial justification likely, print it professionally and use it for every proposal you submit.

Dear Mr..............

Sand Reclamation

Our proposals for installing a Sand Reclamation system in your ...foundry are contained in this folder.

As we understand it, your aim is to reduce the costs of buying in furane sand and resin to a workable minimum, and also to cut the costs of dumping old sand to a minimum.

To achieve both these objectives, we recommend that you install one of our 1tons/hour FU-RECLAIM sand reclamation units with certain additional equipment.

From the calculations we have been able to do, we believe you would get full return on the capital invested in   months. This is without considering Corporation Tax savings coming from 100% first year write-down allowances, or Development Grants if they apply to you. Alternatively, if you choose to lease the FU-RECLAIM equipment or finance it on hire purchase over...   years, you would be saving money from day one without the equipment costing you a penny in real terms. We can, if you wish, introduce you to a number of financial institutions that have regularly helped our customers in the past.

You will see from our prices that we are not the cheapest supplier of sand reclamation equipment. We do not set out to be.

We aim to provide you with a very well-engineered piece of production plant, which will give you the longest possible working life at optimum performance, with the lowest possible maintenance and running costs. It will also be the safest and the quietest sand reclamation system available.

Some idea of the savings on sand, resin, and dumping costs, which you can expect to achieve when you have installed your FU-RECLAIM system, is provided overleaf, followed by the full description, technical specification and prices of the system recommended.

Yours sincerely
John Griffiths
Sales Director

Financial Aspects of Furane
Sand Reclamation using FTL Fu-Reclaim System

Example of savings made by an iron foundry that installed FTL equipment and had previously dumped all old sand and resin.

Foundry using 400 tons per week of furane sand, with an average of 1.4% resin content.

Cost of new sand £10.36 per ton. Cost of resin £720 per ton.

Cost of dumping old sand £3 per ton.

Previous costs per week:

400 tons sand @ £10.36 per ton	£4,144.00
1.4% resin = 5.6 tons @ £720 per ton	£4,032.00
Sand dumping 405.6 tons @ £3 per ton	£1,216.80
Total weekly cost	
	£9,392.80

Total costs per 46 week year
£432,068.80

Costs after installing FTL FU-RECLAIM (operating costs of FU-RECLAIM calculated to be £0.60 per ton of sand reclaimed)

Costs per week:
95 x 4 = 380 tons reclaimed sand @ £0.60 per ton   £ 228.00

1% average resin = 4 ton @ £720 per ton	£2,880.00
5% new sand make up = 20 tons	
@ £10.36 per ton	£ 207.20
5% old sand dumped = 20 tons @ £3 per ton	£60.00
	£3,375.20
Total costs per 46 week year	£155,259.20

Costs saved per week = £6,017.60
Costs saved per year = £276,809.60

Total price of FTL FU-RECLAIM system in this example was £78,000. This included sand silos, pneumatic transporter units, water-cooling system, tower and pumps, installation and commissioning.

Thus, full return on the capital invested is achieved in 13 weeks.

If the FTL equipment had been lease purchased over 3 years with no initial deposit, the repayments of capital and interest would have been about £700 per week, showing a net weekly saving of more than £5,000.

Here is another standard printed page of financial justification, this time for an electric blow-dry hand-dryer against paper and roller towel competition. The next example shows how to justify the change over from roller or paper towels in a business wash room, to ITR electric blower hand dryers.

Assume 100 people only washing their hands once a day, 5 days per week and 48 weeks a year – that is 100 x 5 x 48 = 24,000 hand dries required per year.

For a Roller Towel

A standard roller is 45 yards long; the pull varies between 7 and 9 inches – let us say 8 inches (0.225 yards) and assume only one pull is used for each dry (you know yourself that many people have two pulls) – that is 200 pulls or dries per roll.

The average cost of a roll is £1.40.
The annual cost is thus (24,000 ÷ 200) x £1.40 = £168.00

For Paper Towels

A standard box of paper towels contains 4,800 and costs now £17.68 per box. People use two or three towels to get dry, but just two towels gives 2,400 dries per box.

The annual cost is thus (24,000 ÷ 2,400) x £17.68 = £176.80

For the ITR Wessex Standard

The ITR Wessex Standard with 45 secs timing gives 80 dries per hour. The total cost per dry, comprising electricity costs plus rental cost of the dryer, is estimated at 0.1445p.

The annual cost is thus 24,000 x £0.001445 = £34.68

For the ITR Wessex Commercial

The ITR Wessex Commercial with 36 secs timing gives 100 dries per hour. The total cost per dry, comprising electricity costs plus rental cost of the dryer, is estimated at 0.1156p.

The annual cost is thus 24,000 x £0.001156 = £27.74

That is an annual saving of a minimum of

Roller Towel	£168.00
Standard	£34.68
Saving	£133.32

Or

Roller Towel	£168.00
Commercial	£27.74
Saving	£140.26

Or

Paper Towels	£176.80
Standard	£34.68
Saving	£142.12

Or

Paper Towels	£176.80
Commercial	£27.74
Saving	£149.06

AND THIS IS ONLY FOR 100 DRIES PER DAY

There is no point re-inventing the wheel. Or doing the job the hard way if there is a proven successful easier way. Only your EGO makes you do things your way. Really successful salespeople copy the proven methods of the successful people who have going before them – and improve on those methods.

Chapter 4

How to Get the Facts

Okay, now you know about the format for a good Selling Proposal.

And you're probably wondering how the hell you get the prospective customer to tell you all about his or her Objectives and how you get all the numbers from which you can work out the Financial Justification.

Here we go then. Fasten your lap strap!

Example 1

Situation

You (S) are selling for a shipping agent. You are face-to-face (or over the telephone) with a potential customer (C) who is using one of your competitors.

The dialogue might go as follows:

S. 'How much time do you spend on the paperwork relating to the goods you have to ship, Mr C?

C. 'Ooh, it's got to be a couple of hours every day.'

S. 'If we took it all off your hands and did it all for you, would that be an advantage to you?'

C. 'Well, of course it would.'

S. 'Okay, can I use the savings of this 2 hours a day as the basis of our proposals – and work out some financial projections on this basis – how much money you'll save per year, for example?'

C. 'Well, okay. That sounds fair enough.'

The Customer's Objectives

As we understand it, you are seeking to reduce the average 2 hours per day currently spent completing consignment documentation.

The Financial Justification

Labour costs £8 per hour, including overheads. 2 hours per day x 200 days per year = £3,200 per year. You save ALL this, because we do it all for you. You also have 400 hours time per year available for other, more profitable work.

Example 2

Situation

You (S) are selling Disposable Wet-Wipes to the Head Nursing Sister (C) of an NHS hospital.

The dialogue might go as follows:

S. 'How much time do your nurses spend on the morning patients' bed washing tasks, Sister?'

C. 'Last time we monitored it, it was around 6 nurse hours per ward.'

S. 'How many beds per ward?'

C. 'It averages 18 – fully occupied!'

S. 'If we could reduce that 6 hours per day to, say, 1½ hours per day, would that be significant, Sister?'

C. 'Significant! The nurses abhor that job. Of course it would.'

S. 'Okay, can I use this target saving in time as the basis of our proposals – and do some projections to show how much money you'll save?'

The Customer's Objectives

As we understand it, you are seeking to reduce the daily patient washing operation from the current 6 nurse hours per 18 be ward per day to 1.5 nurse hours per day.

The Financial Justification

Our target saving is 4.5 nurse hours per day per 18 bed ward. At current rates of pay plus overheads this is a saving of £22.50 per day per ward.

You have 20 wards x 365 days per year = £164,250 per year.

The cost of our product would be £9 per week per ward = £9,360 per year.

Your annual saving would thus be £155,000.

You would also have a much happier nursing staff.

Example 3

Situation

You (S) are a manufacturer of printed circuit control panels for burglar alarm systems, selling to a wholesaler (C) who sells all the bits to the local alarm installers.

The dialogue might go like this:

S. 'What's your biggest problem with the control panels you're stocking now?'

C. 'They're more than a bit complicated for our installers customers. We're getting, oooh, around 5 installers every months ringing us up for help – and this kind of hand-holding doesn't bring in a penny of profit, it just takes up our technician's time.'

S. 'How much time, d'you reckon?'

C. 'Probably two or three days a month.'

S. 'So if you could find some simpler control panels which would do the same job or better – and which you could just sell and forget; that your installers could understand easily – would this be of interest to you?'

C. 'Sell and forget. Yes, that's the ticket. I like that.'

The Customer's Objectives

As we understand it, you are seeking control panels which you can 'sell and forget'; i.e. that are so easy to install that there is minimum call back, technical help or customer 'hand-holding', thus saving you time-consuming and unprofitable hassle.

The Financial Justification

Currently out of an average of 15 control panels per month, 5 panels need technical help. This is taking 2.5 days per month of technical time, at £30 per hour = £600 per month cost.

Example 4

Situation

You (S) are trying to sell the manufacture of the product by out-source, instead of, as now, the customer (C) making the product in their own factory. A very political 'out of the frying pan into the fire', high worry risk problem.

The dialogue might go like this:

Hold it. Why am I doing all the work for you? This time, YOU develop the dialogue that will get you the answers that you need to enable you to draft the Customer's Objectives and Financial Justification at the end.

S.

C.

S.

C.

S.

C.

The Customer's Objectives

As we understand it, you are concerned with the number of errors being made in delivering the correct goods, in the correct quantity, at the correct specification and at the correct time.

The Financial Justification

You have estimated that the total cost of errors is currently around £40,000 per year. You have also estimated that, as a direct result of these errors, you are losing around 10 customers per year. Each of these customers gives you an average of £30,000 business per year.

You are, therefore, losing £300,000 business per year due to the error problems, plus the £40,000 direct costs.

Our outside facility will cost you £50,000 per year. This is £15,000 more than it is costing you now to do the work in-house (not including the cost of errors).

We *guarantee* to reduce errors by 60%.

This will logically reduce lost customers by 60%.

On this basis, you will be saving £24,000 of the £40,000 cost of errors and £180,000 of the £300,000 loss of business, for an additional outlay of £15,000

This is a total net gain of £189,000 per year.

Example 5

Situation

Self-explanatory if you read the Customer's Objectives. Have another go at the dialogue.

S.

C.

S.

C.

S.

C.

The Customer's Objectives

As we understand it, you are looking to replace your existing card index system of stock control in your garment warehouse with a computerised system.

Your objectives for such a computerised system are that it should alleviate all the hold-ups, mix-ups and mismatch problems that you are experiencing and which are severely affecting customer relations.

The Financial Justification

You are currently producing 3000 garments per week.

12% of this production is held up in the warehouse due to mix ups with the orders.

At an average cost of £10 per garment, this is £3600 per week held up.

Assume 50% written off because of mismatch of sizes.

The loss per year is, therefore, £90,000.

Due to this problem, you are suffering an average of 2 major cancellations every week. You estimate that this equates to a loss of business per year of around £100,000

Your total losses due to the inadequacy of your present stock control system are therefore around £190,000 per year.

Example 6

Situation

Air conditioning for a 20-employee computer department where the salesperson uses the latest CBI statistics as the basis for the Financial Justification.

Try the dialogue again:

S.

C.

S.

C.

S.

C.

The Customer's Objectives

As we understand it, you are seeking to:
1. reduce absenteeism and staff sickness
2. reduce computer breakdowns to a minimum
3. improve productivity and your working environment.

The Financial Justification

According to the latest CBI survey, the average time off sick per white collar worker is running at 5 days per year.

Sick time should thus be 100 days per year.

With our system, this will HALVE.

The value of these 50 days saved, in terms of productivity, you estimate is around £400 per day x 50 = £20,000 per year.

Computer breakdowns average 6 per year. With our system this will reduce to 2 per year.

The average cost of a breakdown is estimated to be £2000. Annual saving is thus £8000.

Total savings £28,000 per year.

Cost of our system is £8000.

Thus, total pay back is achieved in under 4 months.

Example 7

Finale time! How about this last example to put the salesperson into a classic 'You can't afford NOT to buy' situation?

The Customer's Objectives

As we understand it, you are seeking to minimise the damage to your coils of steel caused by the inadequate handling equipment your people are currently having to use.

You are also seeking a more flexible, more manoeuverable handling system which will enable you to fulfil your customers' goods receiving requirements, something that at present you are unable to do.

Due to the current stop on all capital expenditure, you will need to lease or rent the new equipment necessary to achieve these objectives.

The Financial Justification

You produce 30,000 tonnes of coiled steel per week. The value of this is £100 per tonne on average. You currently scrap 5% due to handling damage. Scrap rate is £30 per 5 tonnes.

Net cost is therefore £105,000 per week of scrapped coils. The cost of the 14 TCLs you need to eliminate ALL this scrap is £280,000.

Pay-back is thus achieved in less than 3 weeks.

Net saving per year will be in the region of £5 million.

As a triple A company, you could lease the 14 TCLs with no initial deposit and at best possible interest rates. Over 5 years, the monthly lease payments would be in the region of £6000 per month.

On this basis, you would be saving around £400,000 per month from month one.

Presenting examples of Customer Objectives

When you and your salesforce colleagues have collected enough specific examples of what your Customers want to do, you can convene a sales meeting and build all your examples into a single A4 page of Customers' Objectives.

What a sales opener this is!

'I've got a list here of the key things our customers have wanted to achieve with our services/products over the past year. Would you run your eye down the list and see if there is anything on it that YOU want to achieve?'

Natural curiosity will do the rest.

Consider my big three reasons for doing the job this way. When you start your sales presentation with the Customer's Objectives List:

1. you switch the customer on by talking about what HE/SHE wants to do, not about what you want to do
2. you open the customer's mind to achieving things he/she hasn't even thought about yet

3. you make it absolutely certain that the customer will want you to quote for the job. And seriously, not just to get rid of you!

Here are three examples, all from real life.

Example 1 – Computer training

Customer's Objectives These are the objectives most of our customers want to achieve. Which of them would also be your objectives?	Priority order
INCREASE the flexibility of your computer training so that you can easily cater for upgrades and alterations to the software.	
INCREASE the availablility of computer training within budgetary requirements.	
INCREASE the quality of computer training within budgetary requirements.	
IMPROVE productivity of new starters.	
IMPROVE the training of staff on new computer systems with minimum disruption.	
REDUCE the time away from work for training purposes.	
REDUCE computer training costs by providing effective, self-paced, 'hands-on' training at the work place or in a classroom.	
REDUCE time taken to fully train staff on a new computer system.	
REDUCE time spent by trainers on repetitious 'low-level' training, thus allowing them to spend more time on a one-to-one basis.	
SAVE time spent in the preparation of computer manuals.	
GAIN the capability to train staff on PC packages as well as your own 'bespoke' system.	

Example 2 – Replacement windows

UNIT 3 WYNDHAM ROAD,
HAWKSWORTH TRADING ESTATE,
SWINDON,
WILTS SN2 1EJ
TEL 0793 618138

Our Customers' Objectives

These are the kind of objectives most of our customers say they want
to achieve. Which of them match YOUR objectives? Can you prioritise
them?

**Priority
order**

INCREASE   the value and thus the saleability of your home

INCREASE   the overall security of your home, against
thieves and vandals which would probably then ...

REDUCE   your home insurance premiums

IMPROVE   the outside and inside appearance of your home

IMPROVE   the comfort you enjoy in your home

REDUCE   the loss of expensive heat

REDUCE   the noise from traffic and neighbours

REDUCE   draughts

REDUCE   the condensation you suffer with your existing
windows

SAVE   a significant proportion of the money you
spend on heating your home and maintaining
it in pristine condition

IMPROVE   extra space to your quality of life

Example 3 – Vending systems

Customer's Objectives These are the objectives most of our customers want to achieve from using our vending systems. Which of them would also be your objectives?	Priority order
INCREASE the range of drinks provided, to include hot, cold and fizzy.	
INCREASE the availablility of drinks provided to a full 24 hours a day.	
INCREASE profitability by covering all costs, including rental of equipment, at 5p vend prices for all drinks.	
IMPROVE the quality of drinks provided.	
IMPROVE the general image and acceptability of vending to your workforce.	
REDUCE the time spent off the job by providing a speedier drinks service.	
SAVE labour by having a fully automated drinks vending service which is maintained solely by us.	
GAIN valuable office space currently taken up by more bulky vending equipment and supplies stores.	
GAIN trade union approval by upgrading the hygiene of your drinks vending service to the highest possible level.	

Second source

The customers' objective in your proposal could sometimes be a single one and fairly general. For example, if you establish that the customer is currently buying *all* his requirements from just one supplier, your proposal could read:

Your Objective

As we understand it, you are currently buying all your requirements from just one supplier.

You are seeking a reliable, quality-orientated, ISO 9000 'second source' supplier to give you cover in the event of any breakdown of supply on the part of your present sole supplier – and to avoid any risk of supplier complacency.

You arrived at this statement of his objectives by more or less putting the words into his mouth during your opening sales presentation.

'What would happen, Mr. Jones, if your present suppliers had a fire, or a strike, and suddenly couldn't maintain your supplies?

How long would it take you to open an account with another supplier and for the new supplier to get things moving? Two months? Could you wait that long without suffering major problems?

If you were already buying, say 20 percent of your supplies from a second supplier, like us, it would be so much easier for you to pick up the 'phone and telephone and get them to increase supplies fast, wouldn't it?

And having two suppliers would keep both of them on their toes, wouldn't it?'

How to quote delivery dates

- **Do Not** state in your proposal, '6/8 weeks'.
- **Do Not** make it even worse by adding 'from acknowledgement of order'.

Instead, find out at the customers' objectives stage of the opening presentation when the customer wants to start using it/wants to change over to you/wants to have it installed.

Even when the customer responds 'It's not important', *YOU give* him a more specific delivery date. 'Well, okay, but I'd like to be a bit more specific, for our own scheduling. How does June 30th grab you for installed and ready to go? Assuming, of course, you are happy to go ahead, anyway.'

What you are aiming for is a statement in your proposal, covering delivery, which reads, for example:

> 'We understand that you would like to have this equipment installed and in operation by June 30th. We can meet this schedule, but to do so we would need to have your order by March 10th at the latest to allow sufficient time for manufacture and commissioning.'

You now have two kinds of sense of urgency – one in the mind of the customer and the other in your mind as you approach March 10th and the order has not been placed.

So you follow up the proposal more effectively, with a very good reason to keep telephoning the customer.

How to make sure you get the first phone call

More and more customers leave placing the order till the last minute, which makes delivery far more important than it should be. The supplier that gets the first phone call from this kind of customer usually wins the order. Here is a way to quote Delivery Dates when you are up against competition that often beats you by quoting a faster time.

> **DELIVERY**
> When it is a life or death situation on in-stock items – 6 HOURS
> For standard items, no rush – 10 DAYS
> For specials average 3 – 4 WEEKS
> *We never lose an order because of delivery.*

That mix of dates, plus the crucial last line! means to the customer that he can get the goods or services faster from you than from anyone else and that you are prepared to be flexible. To the customer who has left it until the last minute, *it is* a life or death situation ... for him. So the customer rings you first. But it leaves YOU in complete control. You can always say NO!

'If we can't get our faxed quotations right, what are we going to do when every customer uses e-mail?'

Chapter 5

Faxed Quotes

More and more customers – especially existing customers – demand that you 'FAX US A PRICE'.

In responding to these demands, the customer is depriving you of the opportunity to do your job of Selling Your Higher Price. He's not doing this deliberately, because he doesn't really know, or care, about anything except how much it is going to cost him next time.

If you know your price is likely to be higher than your competitors, faxing just the basic details is the easiest and the cheapest way of losing the sale. And there's more…

Faxing a quotation or proposal means losing control of both quality *and* the sale. Try to avoid faxing anything as important as a proposal. Better to courier it by same-day motor cycle. Of course, this depends upon the value of the order.

If you *have* to fax a price confirmation or a full proposal (say to an overseas customer) always make sure:

1. that your type size is no smaller than 14pt.

2. that your margins are 30mm minimum both sides and you don't use the top or bottom 20mm of the page.

Then, if the customer's fax machine is grotty, you still stand a good chance that your central message will be clear of the chewed or smudged bits. *Always* follow up a faxed price confirmation with a posted full proposal with all the back-up.

Try to generate a sense of urgency to explain away the brevity of your faxed quote: like the INSTANT RESPONSE QUOTATION, which follows the next, 'everything but the kitchen sink' example:

W.H. BRADY Co Ltd Banbury England   44295268502 > 0295 268502

W.H. BRADY CO. LTD.
Wildmere Industrial Estate ·
Banbury, Oxfordshire OX16 7JU, England
Telephone: (0295) 271291
Fax: (0295) 268502
Telex: 837651 BRADY G

Quotation

Registered Number: 590656 England

Attn: Andy Christie
W H Brady Co Ltd
Wildmere Road
Daventry Road Ind.Estate
Banbury
Oxfordshire
OX16 7JU   United Kingdom

Your Account ref: BRA990
Quote Number: 0940246-1
Please use this reference when ordering

18 Jan 1994

Thank you for your inquiry: Fax dtd 14/1/94   for: Radar MK3 Reflector
We are pleased to submit the following details for your perusal.
If you require further details please do not hesitate to contact us.

'our Drawing: Revision: Date:01/01/00
Product: SCREENPRINTED WITH ADHESIVE
Material:005 Melinex Shiny
          UL/CSA recognised.   Sub Surface Printed. Melinex Polyplate.
Adhesive change to B205   .002" Acrylic P.S.A

Horizontal Size: 304.80 mm Vertical Size: 38.10 mm
Shape: Rectangle   Corner Radius: 0.00 (Square Corners)

Colour	Type of print
RED	Legend
BLUE	Legend
WHITE	Background

Delivery: 10 working days
          from photoproof approval

1 labels per Piece. Packed as 50 Pieces per PACK
We are using same material as we do for the oval label we manufacture for
you - please confirm this is acceptable. Please advise colour references.

Pricing: Qty   Price   Extras: GBP (Sterling)
')   GBP (Sterling) per LABEL   C
          100   1.428   Dietool   0.00
          200   0.891   Setup   62.00
          300   0.712   Colour Match 0.00
          400   0.623   Add'l charges 0.00

Shipping Terms: FOB
****** INTERCOMPANY PRICES ******
We may deliver quantity +/- 10%. Please see Standard Terms.
Samples follow by mail.
For evaluation only. Please supply full details and drawing.

These products will be manufactured to approved BS 5750 Part 2 procedures. Orders less than £100 are subject to a small
order charge of £10.00. Certificates of Conformance are charged at £5.00 per product and sheduled delivery.
Quotation valid for 30 days.

On Behalf of W. H. Brady Co Ltd

Customer Service Special Sales

Last page, 1 page in total

Instant Response Quotation

For the urgent attention of: Andy Christie

From: John Fenton   W. H. Brady Co. Ltd.
                                      Banbury, OX16 7JU

PROJECT/OBJECTIVE

Radar MK3 Reflector Screenprinted labels with adhesive

RECOMMENDATIONS

Same material as the oval label we produce for you, but size 304.80mm wide by 38.10mm high rectangular and adhesive changed to B205

COLOURS	Red, Blue, White (background) Packed 50 labels per pack

PRICE	QUANTITY	PRICE PER LABEL
	100	£1.428
	200	£0.891
	300	£0.712
	400	£0.623
	SETUP:	£62.00

DELIVERY:	10 Working Days from approval of proof

Standard Terms Apply

Need colour references and detailed drawing before we can proceed with production.

Samples and full proposal follow by first class post.

Best regards

The Brady quotation on page 120 is the result of someone trying to get everything onto one single page.

When I use this example with sales people on training sessions, I ask them to quickly tell me what is the product being sold. The answer rarely comes quickly. NEVER use condensed typefaces on a fax, as in the last paragraph. On most continuous roll paper fax machines, this would come out as a blur – unreadable.

Page 121 is my attempt to improve the Brady example, without further reference to Brady. If the example was enlarged to A4 size, the typesize would be 14pt.

Faxing proposals to customers based thousands of miles away is normally the only method open to most suppliers. It is simply too expensive and too time consuming to jump on a plane and take the proposals to a face-to-face meeting.

An overseas courier is by far better than a fax, but if fax is the chosen way, you can still improve your chances of success by laying out your fax so that each key section of the proposal takes up an entirely separate page.

There follows an example of this kind of layout. The product is a computer system for the inter-active training of hospital staff.

FOR THE URGENT ATTENTION OF:		
DATE: FAX:		PAGE: 1
FROM:		OF: 7

FAX

TRAINING SYSTEMS LIMITED

PROPOSAL FOR
BASINGSTOKE DISTRICT HOSPITAL
FOR INSTANT REPLAY TRAINING

Contents

Your Objectives

Our Recommendations

Additional Benefits

Cost Savings

Guarantees and After-Sales Service

TRAINING SYSTEMS LIMITED,

BICESTER HALL,

5 LONDON ROAD, BICESTER 0X6 7BU

PHONE: 0869 323200   FAX: 0869 323201

YOUR OBJECTIVES

As we understand it, your IT training objectives can be divided into immediate, mid/long term and ongoing requirements:

IMMEDIATE. You are seeking to provide a means of rapidly training a wide range of users of the new Electronic Mail system.

MID/LONG TERM. You are seeking to provide initial and continuation training for the introduction of the CASEMIX and any other large scale systems that Basingstoke District Hospital requires.

ONGOING. You are seeking to provide cost effective, quality training for users of all computer applications in the hospital. This would include, but not be restricted to, Office Automation (WP, Spreadsheet and Databases), Finance, Accident and Emergency, PAS, Pathology Age Care and Paediatric.

By establishing a well organised and equipped central training unit which can provide both central and distance learning to all departments within the group, training will become a natural routine, not looked on as a necessary evil.

TRAINING SYSTEMS LIMITED,

BICESTER HALL,

5 LONDON ROAD, BICESTER OX6 7BU

PHONE: 0869 323200   FAX: 0869 323201

OUR RECOMMENDATIONS

Instant Replay will enable you to meet your immediate requirements of training staff on the new "E" Mail system. It will also enable you to carry out your PC WordPerfect training, thus freeing your trainer to carry out other duties, such as developing courseware for new systems. With Instant Replay you will be able to meet mid/long term and ongoing training requirements as it is independent of software and operating systems.

We recommend a start-up package, 20 "Play Only" units, 10 days on-site consultancy, plus various accessories listed later. Based on the figures we discussed on 4th May this will save Basingstoke District Hospital £132,087 in the first year of operation. The detailed figures showing the breakdown of the cost savings are shown in the COST SAVINGS section.

Our recommendations will enable you to train 20 users in a classroom at any one time. The units are portable and can be moved onto wards for night staff training if required. It will also reduce the implementation time for the new hospital systems by reducing the training time necessary to bring people up to scratch on the computers. It is our customers' experience that Instant Replay reduces training time by between 40% and 50% when compared to standard classroom based training. This is because of the repetitious, self-paced nature of the training, combined with the sight, sound and hands-on capability.

TRAINING SYSTEMS LIMITED,

BICESTER HALL,

5 LONDON ROAD, BICESTER OX6 7BU

PHONE: 0869 323200   FAX: 0869 323201

ADDITIONAL BENEFITS

By adopting our recommendations:

- You protect any future investment because Instant Replay operates with all MS-DOS PCs and asynchronous R5232 terminals. This means that your training material and Instant Replay will not have to be upgraded when you change computer systems in the future.

- Instant Replay offers a 24 hour training facility so that night staff can be trained in parallel to day staff.

- You are able to free-up your trainers for re-enforcing the training of those who require more one-to-one attention.

- You have the ability to create customised training for all your computer systems, as well as having access to prerecorded generic training tapes for PC packages so that you do not need to 're-invent the wheel'.

- You will achieve consistent training standards because Instant Replay allows students to repeat the training as often as they need.

- Your staff receive 'hands-on' tuition so that they can immediately practice what they have been taught – 'repetition is the mother of learning'.

- Our customers generally find that production of courseware for Instant Replay is faster than for the standard classroom based training as there is no need to produce additional course material and training aids. Instant Replay can also be used alongside existing training material.

TRAINING SYSTEMS LIMITED,
BICESTER HALL,
5 LONDON ROAD, BICESTER OX6 7BU
PHONE: 0869 323200   FAX: 0869 323201

COST SAVINGS

The training requirement is:

3,600 classroom based training days per year to cover:

> Lotus 123, e-mail,
> CASEMIX,
> WordPerfect
> Nurse management

Training 10 people at a time the costs are:

Trainers time – 2 full time trainers @ £15 per hour	£62,400
Students time – 3,600 days @ £70 per day	£252,000
TOTAL COST	£314,400

Using Instant Replay the costs are:

Trainers time – 1 full time trainer @ £15 per hour	£31,200
Students time – 2,000 days @ £70 per day	£140,000
Instant Replay investment	£55,563
TOTAL COST	£262,763

Costs saved in first year £87,637

TRAINING SYSTEMS LIMITED, BICESTER HALL,
5 LONDON ROAD, BICESTER OX6 7BU
PHONE: 0869 323200   FAX: 0869 323201

The Instant Replay investment includes:

1 x Instant Replay Start Up Package including 2 Instant Replay Units (plus accessories) and three days on-site courseware development…………........................…… £6,290

20 x Instant Replay "Play Only" Units (plus accessories)…. £43,900

5 x Polypropylene Carrying Cases……………………….….. £625

10 days On-site Courseware Creation/Consultancy……..… £4,500

100 x Cassette Tapes – Sony UX6O Type II………………... £180

300 x Cassette Labels (for dot matrix or laser printer)…….. £18

TOTAL INVESTMENT………………………………………….. £55,563

The only additional costs will be travelling and out-of-pocket expenses for the on-site consultancy

THERE ARE NO "HIDDEN" EXTRA COSTS.

Since the life of the equipment is at least 5 years, you may wish to amortise the cost over a 5 year period.

In this instance the annual costs will be:
Trainers time – 1 full time trainer @ £15 per hour	£31,200
Students time – 2,000 days @ £70 per day	£140,000
Instant Replay – 12 months' depreciation	£11,113
TOTAL COST	£182,313

This gives an annual saving of £132,087 and total savings of £660,435 over the 5 year period.

TRAINING SYSTEMS LIMITED,

BICESTER HALL,

5 LONDON ROAD, BICESTER 0X6 7BU

PHONE: 0869 323200 FAX: 0869 323201

Costs saved over the 5 year period	£660,435
Costs saved per year	£132,087
Costs saved per day	£2,540

Thus full return on capital invested is achieved in 22 weeks.

If the Instant Replay equipment is lease purchased over 3 years with no initial deposit, the repayments of capital and interest are about £472 per week, showing a weekly saving of £2,068, FROM WEEK ONE.

GUARANTEES AND AFTER SALES SERVICE

We guarantee that at the end of the Training/Consultancy period, you will have customised INSTANT REPLAY tapes prepared and ready to use for training on your computer system. The only proviso is that you carry out the work between visits, as guided by our Training Consultant.

All equipment is manufactured and tested to the highest standards and is supplied with a 12 month renewable "swap-out" warranty.

We assist with the installation of Instant Replay units. We offer free "hot-line" telephone support. Our philosophy is to look after our customers – WE CARE and help you to gain maximum benefit from your investment in Instant Replay.

End of Transmission

TRAINING SYSTEMS LIMITED, BICESTER HALL,
5 LONDON ROAD, BICESTER OX6 7BU
PHONE: 0869 323200   FAX: 0869 323201

Do we DARE take a really close, critical look at how we quote our customers now?

Chapter 6

How Good (or Bad) Are Your Current Quotations?

This is a checklist for your current Quotations or Proposals. A score of 75 or over should win you the order.

Seventeen different aspects are assessed:

		Maximum Score
1.	Envelope	3
2.	Letterhead	4
3.	Interest	12
4.	Desire	12
5.	Believability	12
6.	Proposition	10
7.	Continuity	3
8.	Language	3
9.	Emotional Appeal	6
10.	Sufficient Information	5
11.	Testimonials	5
12.	Guarantee	8
13.	Ask for Action	4
14.	Make Action Easy	4
15.	Reason to Act Now	4
16.	Check-up	3
17.	Enclosures	2
		———
		100

See the following notes to show how you score.

1. **If the appearance of the envelope is in its favour, score 3 points.**

    Create a good impression on your prospect even before the
    proposal is read. Check the appearance of the envelope and its
    appropriateness for the job. Make certain that there is nothing to
    detract from the effect one is trying to create; nothing that might
    make the prospect arrive at a negative decision before even
    looking inside.

2. **If the appearance of the letterhead will help the sale, score 4 points.**

    The appearance of the letterhead is important. It should give the
    right impression of the kind and character of the business. It
    should not of course be so cluttered that it steals the attention from
    the proposal itself.

3. **If the opening sentence arouses immediate interest, score 12 points.**

    If you don't arouse interest at the very start, the chances of having
    your proposal read through to the end are slim. Be sure to start with
    something of interest to the reader. Do not confuse interest with
    curiosity. The interest should in some way be related to the sales
    story that follows for the proposal to quality for the full 12 points.

4. **If the second and subsequent paragraphs create desire by
    discussing the objectives and the benefits to the prospect,
    score 12 points.**

    Your proposal should not only describe the customer's objectives, it
    should also tell your prospects what the acceptance of your offer will
    do for them – how it will save them time or money, give them useful
    knowledge, add to their comfort. For example, point out to the
    prospects how the purchase will add to their own expertise.
    Description alone of a product or service doesn't always create
    desire.

5. **If the reasons for buying are convincing and the proposal has
    believability, score 12 points.**

    Certainly everything is lost if your proposal lacks conviction and believability. You may have an excellent product or service, selling at a reasonable price, but if your proposal contains statements that your prospects simply cannot accept you will not be doing justice to your offer. Would you buy on the basis of what you have read in the proposal?

6. **If your proposition is a good one, score 10 points.**

You must build your sales proposition on a firm foundation. Your sales story must offer something the prospect can use. It must be at a fair price that can be afforded. Again, the best way to test this is to try it out on yourself.

7. **If each paragraph leads you on to the next, and the next, giving the proposal continuity, score 3 points.**

The sections of the proposal must fit together to make one complete unit. Every part must develop out of the preceding one and lead into what follows. A proposal that consists merely of a number of completely separate paragraphs will sound jerky and will fail to hold the reader's attention. Make the proposal smooth reading.

8. **If you have written in the language of the average prospect, score 3 points.**

By writing in the language of the average prospect it means using any known peculiarities of speech common to the industry or the particular classification of recipient. To illustrate, you would talk in one vein to mechanics and in an entirely different way to farmers and in yet another way to housewives. If there is no accepted language for your prospect, score the appropriate points anyhow.

9. **If you have used an appropriate emotional appeal: love, duty, pride, gain, self-indulgence or fear, score 6 points.**

Your sales proposal should present your proposition in logical and reasonable terms so that your prospect can understand it clearly. But reason alone is not a strong enough argument. If possible, appeal to your prospect's emotions. Make his mouth water, figuratively. Tempt him through the use of working words and descriptive phrases. Make him want and be eager to have what your product will do for him.

10. If you have given the prospect sufficient information to enable him to make a decision with regard to after sales service, back up support, etc, score 5 points.

Make your story complete. Give your prospect all the information needed to decide whether or not the product is of interest and should be acquired. If you don't take the trouble to complete your sales story the reader will not do it for you.

11. If you have used a good testimonial, score 5 points.

A testimonial is a very powerful selling tool. If you can get endorsements from people who are in a position to lend prestige to your offer, use them.

12. If your proposal contains a guarantee of satisfaction, score 8 points.

If your proposal is soliciting a direct order it should by all means contain a guarantee of satisfaction. This will make your offer more convincing and demonstrate that you are acting professionally and in good faith. Thus, if your proposal contains a guarantee or one is not appropriate, allow yourself the 8 points.

13. If you have asked for some definite action, score 4 points.

Don't leave the prospect in the air after finishing the proposal. Ask him to take a definite step – send in an order form, request further information, send for a sample. This will keep your offer alive and place you in a better position to take appropriate follow-up steps.

14. If you have made it easy for the prospect to act or you will be taking the proposal to the prospect yourself, score 4 points.

Include the means for taking action in your mailing piece. If you want your prospect to send in orders, provide an easy-to-use order form plus a postage-free reply envelope.

15. If you have given a good reason or inducement to act now, score 4 points.

The time element will work against you unless you urge your prospects to act without delay. When your prospects put off acting on your offer, there's always the possibility that they will go cold on your proposition entirely.

16. If you have read the proposal aloud, given it to someone else to read, to criticise, or slept on it, score 3 points.

Three habits worth cultivating. Each enables you to view your proposal as a typical prospect, not as the author. The brief time required for these steps often highlights omissions that slip by during the original preparation. If you adopted any one of them on the particular proposal being evaluated, you are entitled to the 3 points.

17. If you are enclosing a folder, circular, or other sales literature with the proposal, score 2 points.

With every proposal, some form of supporting sales literature is almost invariably needed. (Ensure it's up to date and not dog-eared.) This gives you a chance to go into impressive detail in describing your offer. On some types of proposal, the enclosure may not be needed and, if that is the case, you can still give your proposal the 2 points.

135

Changing over to your New Proposal Style

It'll take a while to get it right. On jobs in the pipeline you won't have all the information you need. But there is nothing in the rulebook that says you can't submit a second, better quotation, if you have enough data to improve on the first one.

It really impresses a prospective customer to have a salesperson telephone and say – 'We've been giving your problem a lot of thought since we submitted our quotation and we've come up with some extra data which makes the deal we're offering even more attractive. I've prepared a second proposal, which contains all this extra data. Can I come in and go through it with you? How about Tuesday at 9.50, or would early afternoon be better for you?'

And now you are in a position to use the ultimate gambit – a technique that really gets you some fun out of the job, at the expense of your competitors.

During the weeks you are perfecting this UWC format for your proposals (about the time you stop calling them quotations), you take some copies of the UWC instruction sheet over to your own purchasing department and you encourage your company's buyers to use the set of instructions on all their suppliers and prospective suppliers. It will halve their enquiry/quotation processing time and make sure they select the best value for money deal for your company, every time.

You arm yourself with another dozen copies of the set of instructions, this time with your company's name on the top, not UWC.

Now you can apply the ultimate gambit. You take in your proposal to go through it with a prospective customer. You go through it in the way we've already described. At the end, you close with the two most powerful questions in Selling:

'Are you happy with everything?'
'Can we go ahead then?'

If he says, 'Yes; don't see why not', you don't need to play your ace.

But if he says, 'Not yet; I'd better wait until the other quotations come in, so that I can compare them with yours', it's time for your ace.

> 'You've no doubt noticed, Mr Jones, our proposal is quite a lot different from most quotations you see. *(Pause: get an affirmative.)* It follows the format we use in our own purchasing department when we go out to suppliers for quotations. Our buyers send out a set of instructions to all our suppliers and prospective suppliers, telling them precisely how to quote.
>
> By doing this, they have three or four identical format quotations to consider; they can therefore compare like with like and they can guarantee to select the best all-round offer every time, and much faster.
>
> How do the other quotations you've received so far measure up to ours? *(It's nice if you're first and he hasn't received any of the others yet, but no matter...)*
>
> Can I make a suggestion?... *(and here you bring out half a dozen of your purchasing department's instruction sheets).*
>
> Why don't you try this for yourself? Send one of these – with your name on top, of course – to each of the other suppliers that are quoting on this job, and see how much easier it will be for you to compare the quotations and come to a decision. Have you got time in your schedule to do this?'

If he's got the time, he'll do it. It's irresistible. If he hasn't got the time, you've still made a friend, given him something to try out on his next job, and enhanced your chances of getting this particular order. (Your idea is worth 10% on price as a consultancy fee!)

So now you see the reason for the introductory story. Your competitors are now the ones crying – 'Who the hell do these people think they are – telling us how to quote!' – they will lose by default. Some will completely ignore the instructions. All will have to do the survey again because they didn't ask the right questions first time round.

If only you could be a fly on the wall in their sales office when those instructions arrive out of the blue.

But don't forget who else might be reading this!

How to use the Proposal to set up a Demonstration

When you go through that Proposal with your prospective customer, he will not agree with everything you've said every time. Sometimes he'll be doubtful on some major or minor point. Sometimes it will be a doubt based on an inability to understand fully – and you won't get very far by telling him, or even inferring, that he's thick!

Sometimes, the doubt will be based on a misunderstanding.

Whatever; you clear up the doubt if you can, and keep going. If you can't clear it up, set it to one side, and secure complete agreement on everything else.

Then try a different close. 'You're happy with everything except this one doubt on the crushing capabilities, then, Mr Jones?' Get his agreement to this. Then move on. 'So if we can clear up this doubt to your complete satisfaction, may I assume you'll go ahead?'

It'll be very difficult for him to say 'No'. Worst you're likely to get is – 'All other things considered, I wouldn't be surprised.'

So you propose a demonstration – at your works or at one of your customer's premises, or whatever is most appropriate. A demonstration with one clear-cut objective in mind – to clear up that doubt. The best kind of demonstration, as you'll see in the next chapter.

And if there are a number of decision-makers and influencers involved in the project, your last question should be – 'Can we get Mr Brown, and Miss Smith and Mr Humphries to attend the demonstration? We could lay on a tour of our works at the same time'.

Would YOU buy it, if you were the Customer?

This is the acid test for a Proposal. And the measure of a really professional salesperson. That he or she can put himself or herself into the customer's shoes; really into the customer's personality and working situation; empathise with the customer; read through the Proposal before it's taken in and answer honestly and truthfully – 'Would I buy this, if I were this customer?'

Would you really? Why would you? Think about the reasons in detail. Think about *all* the reasons why you would buy it.

Then go in and *sell* it – with more confidence and sincerity than you'd ever dreamed you could muster. You'll do it, you'll be convincing, because now ... you believe.

Go in and *sell* it, because you've thought out exactly what best to do – and why.

And if you find yourself answering 'No, I don't think I would buy it if I were him' – tear the Proposal apart and do it again until you can answer truthfully, 'Yes, I'll buy it now'.

The best selling word in Selling is

SOLD

Chapter 7

Meeting Your Customers' Expectations

This chapter gives you examples for the fifth and final section of your Selling Proposal - where you need to provide PROOF positive of how good a supplier you are, and have been in the past.

You need to live up to your future customers' expectations by re-living your past successes. Customer expectations keep increasing remorselessly, in spite of recessions and in spite of whatever you do, or have done, to improve quality and service.

Never, never take a customer for granted.

McGraw Hill conducted a major survey not so long ago to establish the reasons why customers changed suppliers. They discovered that 60 per cent of customers who changed suppliers did so *not* because of any failure or reduction in quality, *nor* because of price, but because *they felt they were being taken for granted.*

Do not assume that a customer will know about your products or services, your company, the people you do business with. You need to *tell them.* You need to remind them regularly.

Another key point: the best selling word in Selling has always, until recently, been **NEW.** The second best selling word in Selling has always been **SOLD.**

But in a lot of industries, like I.T., these top two words are now reversed. **SOLD** is now the best selling word. **NEW** is not so important. Customers no longer want to be innovators, at the leading edge of technology, guinea pigs. Customers today want to know who *else* has bought the product or service and how well and how reliably it is performing.

In this respect, Client Lists and Testimonial Letters are the gold bricks of the New Millennium.

Testimonials

How many good, useable letters from customers are buried in the files, forgotten and never to be seen again?

Dig them out. Send copies (at least 10 of each) to every salesperson. Provide display albums so that they can use the letters professionally. Add at least three customer letters to every Proposal.

How many good, useable letters from customers are there in your salespeople's files, jealously guarded, for their eyes only! Who the hell do they think they are in competition with - their own colleagues? Their own company? Get hold of those letters and circulate them to every salesperson.

A testimonial letter doesn't have to be written directly to the person using it. Any letter to any person in the company that says, 'We are very pleased with what you have done for us', is effective proof anywhere and the most powerful closing tool you can get.

Targets

Set each of your salespeople a target and make things happen. Each salesperson must secure one new testimonial letter every month. No excuses.

After six months you will have enough letters to build them into a special brochure - 'What the Customers Say' - about your business.

Produce a new brochure with a new set of letters every six months - and eclipse your competitors.

Getting Testimonials

Your Managing Director is the best person to procure maximum response. As much as 80% is not unusual. Not all the replies will be good but you need to know about the bad news as well. Consider the following example:

IMO Precision Controls Limited
1000 North Circular Road
Staples Corner
London NW2 7JP

Telephone 0208 452 6444
Fax 0208 450 2274

Dear John,

Your company is a valued customer for IMO Jaguar drives, and I thank you for your custom during the past years.

As we enter the new financial year, with all of our new products in stock, I want to make sure that we are giving our customers the best service we possibly can. For that reason I write to ask you if you would be kind enough to drop me a line to tell me what you think of us as a supplier:-

· Are we living up to your expectations?
· Are we doing everything you expect from us?
· Is there anything more that you would like us to do?
· Could we be doing more for you?
· How much do you value our 5 year warranty?

It's vital feedback like this from our customers which enables the Jaguar team and me to make sure we are steering the business in the right direction, and to make sure our systems and practices are meeting the needs of the customers.

Your response would be extremely valuable. Thank you in anticipation,

Yours sincerely

Edward W G Kirk
Division Director.

VAT Registration No. 346 7454 32
Reg. Office 1000 North Circular Road
London NW2 7JP
Registered in England No. 770038

ISO9002

The testimonial letters you receive (only after you have asked for them) come in all shapes and sizes. Here is one I did ask for, from a company you've heard of before.

TSL **Training Systems Limited**

Technology based training products and services

Telephone: 0869 323200
Fax: 0869 323201

John Fenton Stratagems plc
Clifford Hill Court
Clifford Chambers
STRATFORD UPON AVON
Warwickshire CV37 7QT

Dear John,

Thank you very much for your advice at the 'Quoting' masterclass yesterday. The whole day was packed full of ideas; and we have already produced our first quotations along the lines recommended!

I have produced our Criteria For Ordering and Customer Objective sheets and would be grateful for any feedback that you may have on them.

I look forward to attending your future masterclass seminars! With best wishes.

Yours sincerely,

Len Stafford
Managing Director

Some are great all through - like the example above. Others are what I call 'YES BUT' letters. They contain a few words which destroy the credibility of the overall letter.

With these, you can extract the bit you want to use and leave out the rest. The extract, always with the name and company of who wrote the words, you can build into your Customer List, like the example from Learning Connection (overleaf).

PROFILE

Improving the performance of people at work

Client List

AA Insurance Services Ltd
Adlestones (Jewellers) Ltd
Allied Maples
Augustus Barnett
Beales
W Boyes and Co Ltd
Brahm Advertising
British Gas plc
British Shoe Corporation

> " We commissioned the Learning Connection to design, develop and implement a Customer Care training package for Shoe City staff.
>
> The quality of the training package in terms of content and presentation was very professional. The combination of our business knowledge and their expertise in the service sector, ensured we had a programme that met the needs of our people.
>
> It would be remiss of me not to acknowledge the involvement that was so readily and enthusiastically given on a personal basis to us during the project and for this we thank you very much. "
>
> **Declan Gormley, General Manager, British Shoe Corporation**

British Steel Corporation
C & A
Co-operative Retail Services
Cumbrian Co-operative Society
Eaden Lilley
Elphicks of Farnham
Essilor Ltd
Esprit Ltd
Harcros Timber & Building Supplies Ltd
ICL
IKEA
Independant Insurance Company
Invicta Co-operative
Jarrolds
K Shoe Shops Ltd

> " It is the best diagnostic analysis from a consultant which we have read on Retailing. It has galvanised us into immediate action. We are most grateful to you and your team for such excellent work "
>
> **Tim Lewis, Managing Director, K Shoe Shops**

Legal & General
Lewis's
Lincoln Co-operative Society
The Littlewoods Organisation
Lowndes Queensway
Midland Electricity Board Plc
Makro
Newcastle Breweries Ltd
Newcastle City Council
Nokia Mobira
Northern Ireland Civil Service
North Yorkshire Co-operative Society
Olympus Sport International
Plymouth and South Devon Co-operative Society
Sears Group
Selfridges
Sigma Training
Swansea City Council
Superquinn
Tagus
Toray Textiles
TSB Plc
W H Smith Do It All

> " Do It All has worked with The Learning Connection for a number of years in various capacities. During this time, we have been impressed with their professionalism and knowledge and they have helped us considerably. They played a major part in the implementation of our Customer Care training programme (First Service) which has been very successful. We have been particularly impressed with their desire to provide us with exactly what we require - a rare commodity in external training organisations! "
>
> **David Tomkinson, Staff Training Manager, W H Smith Do It All**

Wendy Wools
Whitbread & Co Ltd
Yorkshire Water Services

> " I would like to take this opportunity to thank you and your staff for the highly professional way in which the sessions were conducted.
>
> Your ability to tailor the 'Inside Story' package to the specific needs of our organisation considerably enhanced it's value and utility.
>
> The way in which you were able to tune into our culture was also of considerable benefit and is so often not the case with some consultants"
>
> **Trevor Drury, Customer Service Manager, Yorkshire Water**

Supplier Evaluation Reports

If you have ever been asked, out of the blue, for a Supplier Evaluation Report, you'll already know how impossible it is to deliver the customer's request. And if you don't conform, you don't even get onto the customer's list of pre-approved suppliers.

SERs are particularly the forte of OEM (Original Equipment Manufacturer) customers. All they are seeking to do is to protect themselves. They need to know that you'll still be there, giving them good products and good service in five year's time.

Boy Scout rules! Be prepared. Put your own SER together *before* you are asked for one. Then use it on every sales opportunity. Add it to every quotation and proposal. Then, if you are the only supplier doing this, the customers will start asking your competitors for their SER. A significant edge for maybe a year when you are selling at a higher price.

Here is an example of a Supplier Evaluation Report. It is based on the SER used by Plessey group and adopted by the Institute of Purchasing Management in its 'guidelines to members'.

SUPPLIER EVALUATION REPORT

(Plessey)

Supplier:..................

Contract:..................   Date:....................

Reasons for asking for all this information.

When suppliers have to fulfil contracts over a lengthy period, customers must be certain that there is negligible risk of the suppliers going broke; that suppliers do not become over dependent on one customer and can finance the cost of producing to the customer's schedules and also finance expansion of facilities if this is necessary. A supplier's plans for growth need to dovetail closely into a customer's plans for increasing his business with that supplier. Pricing policies must demonstrate a supplier's awareness of the need for profit, rather than be based on initial marginal costings designed to secure a contract, with higher prices to follow.

All these things the professional purchasing executive must establish before orders are placed. The questions that follow in this Supplier Evaluation document are designed to establish these facts. Please answer all questions accurately; there is no future for the relationship between customer and supplier if a false picture is presented at the very beginning of the relationship.

THE COMPANY
Full Name:
Registered Office:
Headquarters:
How long in present business:
Spares and Service Depots and Sales Offices:
(give all addresses)

OWNERSHIP
Type of Company - Private or Public:
Directors:
Shareholders:
(majority holding first)
Subsidiary interests:
(or other divisions)
If group, please draw family tree.
Continue on separate sheet if necessary.

MANAGEMENT
Please list names and extent of experience of those executives relevant to this contract and to general customer relations.

FINANCIAL

Please provide last Annual Report and Chairman's Statement if this is available, or Company Profile literature.

Last 3 years performance:

Turnover   Profit   Return on Capital   Gearing Ratio

Next 5 years projection of turnover: (excluding price increases)

Terms of Payment:

Quantity Discount Structure:

FACILITIES

Does the Company manufacture, assemble or distribute its products? (those applicable to the contract).

If it assembles or distributes, where are the products manufactured?
      Country of Origin:
      Name of Manufacturer:

Number of employees: **now**   **3 years ago**
      Production:
      Administration:
      Sales force:
      Service force:

Nature of production equipment:

Nature of accounting and administrative equipment/systems:

If you use computers, which kind and for what?

Quality Assurance, testing and inspection facilities:

Government, Ministry of Defence or other Approvals:

MARKETS AND CUSTOMERS

What proportion of your total turnover comes from the products you are quoting for on this contract?

How do you see this proportion changing over the next 5 years?

From what kind of companies/industries does most of this business come?

Please give the names, addresses, telephone numbers and contacts of 3 current customers whom we can contact to ask about the service they get from you and the reliability of your products.

Educating the Customer

The final example in this chapter on Proof is a Range List.

Many customers only buy one or two things from you and are not aware of everything else you can supply. So to end your Selling Proposals with a page like this is part of their education and very good sense.

EXAMPLE PRODUCT RANGE LIST
FENNER SALES AND SERVICE
MAIN PRODUCTS

BEARINGS
Metric and Inch
Ball, Roller and Thrust Bearings
E.T.N. Roller
Timken and SKF Tapered Roller
High Performance Spherical Roller
SL Full Complement
Split Roller, Transmission
Needle Roller, Linear and Dry Plain
Nickel Plated Self-Lube Housings
Cast Steel GPK Plummer Blocks

MAIN STOCKISTS OF
RHP, SKF, INA, SNFA, TIMKEN,
GLACIER, OILITE BUSHES

OIL SEALS
Greases, Adhesives, Sealants

POWER TRANSMISSION
Wedge Belts, V-Belts, Flat Belting
Synchronous Drives
Taper Lock Pulleys and Bushes
Taper Lock Hubs and Adaptors
Shaft Couplings
Universal Joints

ROLLER CHAIN & SPROCKETS

GEARBOXES
Inline Helical, Worm,
Helical Worm, Bevel Helical
Shaft Mounted Speed Reducers
Spiral T,
With or Without AC or DC Motors

GEARBOX SERVICE
Repairs and Modifications Fenner,
Rossi, Opperman

ELECTRIC MOTORS
AC, DC, Single Phase, Three
Phase.
Base Places, Slide Rails

ELECTRIC MOTORS
AC Inverters, DC Controllers
Electronics Softstarts
Electronics Shearpins

PNEUMATICS
Hoses, Tubes & Fittings
Valves, Cylinders, FRLs

*'400 competitors were
undercutting us on price by
margins of 20% or more.*

*Then you came along and helped
us develop our CFO List and
our new sales format for Sales
Proposals and showed our
sales force how to use them.*

*Now we have an edge
not one of our 400 competitors can beat.'*

Ian Garner

Managing Director

The Hobart Mfg Co Ltd

Chapter 8

Why Do People Buy From Us?

If you conducted a survey across your entire customer base and asked every single customer the question 'What Criteria for Ordering did you use when you selected us as your supplier?' or 'What factors did you consider most important to you when you decided to choose us as your supplier?' you would develop a pretty long list of reasons, which you could then refine into your Number 1 Ace Selling Tool for selling your higher price - your CFO List.

Or you could take a short cut and still achieve the same objective. One called ……..

A day's worth of USP

USP stands for UNIQUE SELLING POINT. It was all the rage before someone invented the word 'Marketing' and fudged everything.

USP is the difference, the edge you've got over your competitors. It's likely to be different for each product or service, against each competitor. If you don't know - in fine detail - what your USP is, then you can't sell successfully against competition.

Finding out what your USPs are, if you are a sales manager, also gives your salesforce all that essential knowledge they need, from which they build their confidence. A fuller explanation of USPs and the procedures a sales manager can adopt to establish them is set out in the first section, Selling: The Most Important Job in the World.

For your CFO List, you need the things which are clearly your USPs, plus a selection of things where you are just as good as any of your competitors - because when you use your CFO List to back up a proposal, your competitors will not be there. You use your key USPs in your main face-to-face presentation, of course.

Now, all you individual salespeople out there - don't wait for your sales manager to call the meeting. Get cracking yourself. The meeting might never happen otherwise, and that's a hell of a lousy reason to stay ignorant.

CFO Lists are highly copiable. You don't have to re-invent the wheel. If anyone else's USP fits your situation - and is *fact,* not fiction - then borrow it and build it into your CFO List.

For this purpose, there follow a few more examples of CFO Lists that I have developed for other kinds of suppliers.

CFO Example 1

James Dubois & Co.
Chartered Accountants and Registered Auditor
Lynnwood Road, Epsom, Surrey KT1 4LF

CLIENT REASONS
These are some of the reasons most of our clients deal with us:

PRICE - We give you real value for money. This means we hardly ever lose a client because of price.

RELIABILITY - We produce your work when you need it.

QUALITY - Our aim is to give you the best - Total Quality Management for a quality service

RESPONSE - We're quick and efficient: delays cost you money and cause inconvenience

PROBLEM SOLVING - We're here to solve your problems.

COMPETENCE - We get your work right with the minimum disruption to your business.

PERSONAL SERVICE - Our people are there when you need to talk or meet with them. We're convenient; we all know the clients and we react quickly.

HELPFUL - When we ask our clients why they deal with us, they say: 'Because we like the people; they know their stuff; they're helpful; they're happy; they try harder'.

PHILOSOPHY - We put our clients FIRST. We CARE

CFO Example 2

Powersport International Ltd

CRITERIA FOR ORDERING (CFO)

These are the reasons most of our customers buy from us.
How many of these reasons would feature on YOUR CFO list?

Price
We give the very best value for money

Delivery
We keep our promises

Quality
All our equipment is 'Squaddy Proof'. We don't have BS5750 because since 1975 we've had AQAPS Edition 1, the NATO/MOD Quality Assurance Certification

Service Response
Quick and efficient. No delays which cost you money or inconvenience your customers

Competence
We get your orders right with minimum paperwork

Reliability
We have a fully documented record of product performance which proves longer working life

Running Costs
Lowest possible

Maintenance Costs
Lowest possible

Performance
Maximum possible on a consistent basis

Safety
Our equipment meets all current and proposed CEN safety regulations

Communications
We are easy to do business with. Our people are easy to get hold of when you want to talk to them

Finance
We help you to find the money to buy the best equipment

Philosophy
We put our customers FIRST. WE CARE

CFO Example 3

The Tennant Rubber Co Ltd

These are the principle reasons our customers buy from us.

How many of these reasons feature on YOUR list of factors that you look for when you are choosing suppliers?

PRICE	We do our best to give you the very best value for money
QUALITY	Both in product and specification
RELIABILITY	Systems conformance with ISO 9000
LEADING EDGE SUPPLIER	We keep you informed of new product development which gives you even better value for money
ONE-STOP SHOPPING	Around 1700 products in stock - plus we do specials FAST
EASY TO DO BUSINESS WITH	Competent, knowledgeable staff who put YOU first
PROBLEM SOLVING	And they are technically competent too
WE DO THE LEG WORK	If we haven't got it we'll find it for you
NICE PEOPLE	Nice people
COMPANY PHILOSOPHY	OUR AIM IS TO SELL GOODS THAT DON'T COME BACK, TO PEOPLE WHO DO

CFO Example 4

Training Systems Ltd

CRITERIA FOR ORDERING (CFO)

These are the reasons most of our customers buy from us. How many of these reasons would feature on YOUR CFO list?

PRICE	We give the best value for money.
DELIVERY	We keep our promises.
QUALITY AND RELIABILITY	All our equipment is 'Squaddy Proof' and has a renewable swap-out warranty.
PROBLEM SOLVING	We provide telephone advice throughout the life of our equipment (AT NO ADDITIONAL COST).
CLASSROOM OR WORK PLACE TRAINING	We provide economical and effective computer training for any situation, whether in the classroom, at the workplace, or at remote locations.
ONE-STOP SHOP	We can provide all you computer application training requirements, from PC to Mainframe, standard packages or bespoke software.
SAFETY	Our equipment meets all current and proposed safety regulations.
COMMUNICATIONS	We are easy to do business with, our people are easy to get hold of when you want to talk to them.
FINANCE	We help you finance the product in the way that is best for you.
PHILOSOPHY	We put our customers first. WE CARE!

CFO Example 5

Arden
COMPUTER SERVICES
LIMITED

Why Our Customers Choose Us

These are the top ten reasons why more than 1200 businesses have bought computer systems from Arden since June 1992.

How many of these ten feature on YOUR Criteria for Ordering list?

1. Price   We give the Best all round Value for Money.

2. Delivery   We keep our promises.

3. One-stop shopping   We can supply everything you'll need. We're a TOTAL SOLUTION dealer.

4. Quality   We won the IBM Quality Award in 1991. We have ISO 9002 (BS5750).

5. Training   We teach your people, hands on, how to get the best out of your systems.

6. Technical expertise   We give fast 'HOT LINE' support. Most maintenance - preventative, under contract or emergency is handled by our own engineers.

7. Nice people   Time after time, when we ask our customers why they prefer to buy from Arden, they say 'Because we like the people. They know their stuff; they're helpful; they're happy; they try harder.'

8. We'll be there   Fast, in response to your needs - and also in 2094, because we are part of the £2.4 billion AMEC Group, not a struggling, stand-alone small business.

9. Finance   We help you find the money to buy the best system to meet your objectives.

10. Philosophy   We put our customers first. We CARE.

In selling, there are no prizes
for coming second.

Winning is EVERYTHING.

So why keep taking chances?

Chapter 9

If You Want To Win, Take It In

What to do when there's just you and the decision-maker

When you do business on a one-to-one basis, just you and your customer's key decision-maker, have you ever asked yourself why he or she asks you for a quotation or a proposal in writing when you've just done the best selling job in your life?

Okay, if you're up against strong competition, they are going to compare your deal with someone else's. Maybe they are going to play Dutch auctions. So you need a Proposal, not a quotation.

But what if you're not up against competition? Why do they want a quotation or proposal from you then? Maybe because they've got just so much money to spend, and a number of different things they could spent it on. So they wants to be sure they're spending the money on the thing that'll do their business the most good. So you need a

Proposal, not a quotation.

There are other reasons, however. The sneakier reasons. They just don't want to go ahead yet, and they're stalling for time. They aren't sure and want time to think it over. They have decided 'No', but lack the guts to tell you 'No' - so instead they say, 'Okay, looks promising. Send me a quotation and I'll consider it and let you know.'

Or maybe it's because they have always done business that way, or it's Company policy always to have a record of things bought, before they're bought, in case things go wrong and they need someone to blame. (Someone other than themselves!)

Or maybe you tender a quotation because it's your company policy, whether the customer asks for one or not.

Whatever the reason, you'll do more business, win more orders, if you submit a Proposal, not a quotation.

And when you have gone to the trouble of preparing a good Proposal and you're selling on a one-to-one basis, there is one absolutely critical golden rule:

If you want to win – take it in.

Don't send the Proposal through the post. Okay, if you have to, you still have a better chance of winning if you're up against competition and the customers want to compare two or more deals and decide which is best - it won't just be a question of price if you present them with a Proposal and your competitors send them quotations. But for all the other situations I've mentioned - if you want to win, take it in. Telephone and make a firm appointment:

> 'Morning, Mr Jones. We've completed our proposals and I'm ready to bring them in and go through them with you. I'd like to do this rather than post them to you, just to make absolutely sure we've got everything right. Would tomorrow morning suit you, or would you prefer the afternoon, say, about 4.30pm?'

The very best competitive salespeople stick to their guns even when the customer replies - 'I'm very busy just now. Put it in the post, will you?'

'With respect, Mr Jones, it's very important to us that we've got everything right, and I think it's very important to you. We're talking about being able to save you something like £27,000 a year. If this week's out, how about next week? I'd rather lose a week and make sure we've interpreted your requirements absolutely correctly. How does next Wednesday look, I'm within fifteen miles of you in the afternoon?'

So you take it in. Top copy for the customer, a copy for you, in case you need to make amendments, and the file copy. And you take the customer through the Proposal from start to finish, getting agreement to everything you've said, step-by-step.

'When we conducted the survey, Mr Jones, you said these were the Objectives you wanted to achieve. (Go through the list of customer's objectives at beginning of Proposal.) Now, are these objectives still valid, or has anything happened since our survey to change them in any way?' (Pause: count silently to five, wait for his okay or information on changes. If changes, decide whether you can proceed or instead gather new information and re-submit the Proposal.)

It's incredible how quickly things change in any kind of business. How do you find out whether your listed Objectives are still valid if you post the Proposal?

Assuming the Objectives are still valid, you get their agreement to your list, then you move on to Your Recommendations. Once again, get their agreement that the way you are proposing the job should be done meets with their approval - and that they fully understand how their objectives will be achieved.

Move on to the Summary of Benefits. Again, get their agreement to your list. Then into the Financial Justification. Go through the calculations and projections, making sure they agree with the figures and that you haven't exaggerated at all (a good basis is never to assume more than 80% of what you *know* you can do for them). At the end of this section, ask them, 'Are these kind of savings what you are looking for, or should we see if we can get more?' Your figures are likely to be a lot *more* than they were hoping for, so they'll probably say, 'No, they look fine to me.' So you have agreement on the Justification.

One more step to go. Through the guarantee and after-sales service section. Through the third-party references. Agreement on this last section.

Both of you lean back in your chairs. 'Fine, Mr Jones. Thank you very much for going through it all with me. You're happy with everything then?'

He can't say 'No'. He can't even say 'Maybe'. He's said 'Yes' to every section in the Proposal. He can only say 'YES', now.

So you have the Proposal's wonderfully simple *built-in, automatic close...*

'Can we go ahead, then?'

And he ain't got no place to go!

PS. Take in three copies of the Proposal. One for him. One for you. And one for the Joker! That's the person you didn't even know exists whom he wants to run it past before going ahead. And he's never in when you are there. So you need a copy for him. This will impress your Decision Maker immensely. Don't penny pinch; it is only pennies.

What to do when there's you, your contact and his boss

This is why *most* people you sell to ask you for a quotation. They aren't the person who makes the decision. Often they never tell you this, because they feel they'd deflate their egos if they did. Some are simply full of their own self-importance, building their own empires, and have lost sight of the real reason they are there - which is to get the best deal they can for their company, make it as efficient as possible, save as much money as they can, whichever fits their job specification.

Where you should be selling to the boss, you find yourself selling to the delegated representatives. And the delegated representatives will never let you through to talk direct to the boss.

So you have to sell to your contacts and they then have to persuade the boss that the deal is a good one. *They're your classic unpaid, untrained, unmotivated amateur salespeople.*

Think about the problems. What do you want your contacts to talk to the boss about? Which benefits do you want them to stress? What kind of things will turn the boss on - and turn the boss off?

What ammunition do you give your contacts to help them sell the deal to the boss? They have your sales brochures, your specification sheets, but will they be able to find them when they get the opportunity to talk to the boss? Will they even bother to look?

You told them in detail about the benefits and you worked out for them how much better the deal should be in financial terms, didn't you? But will your contacts remember much of this when they get to talk to the boss? Not likely!

More often than not, it will be just your Proposal contacts use when they're trying to sell a deal to the boss, plus what they can remember of what you told them when you were face-to-face, which won't be much.

Just imagine, therefore, what sort of job they do if all you've given them is the traditional legal Quotation document.

If you want to win with a delegate representative, *take it in.* It's your only chance to give your unpaid, untrained, unmotivated salesperson a crash course on what to do and say about the proposal, to the boss. Here is a table of statistics on *recall* - the amount people remember of information conveyed to them after varying periods of time. There are three methods listed for the way the information is conveyed - the three methods we all use when we are Selling.

165

You can see clearly from this table how important it is to communicate properly - using all the senses, using your voice and appropriate visual aids. A sales presentation conducted with just the voice and no visual aids whatsoever is the worst of all when it comes to remembering afterwards what was said. Just pictures and no voice at all is better than just the voice.

Method of conveying information	PERCENTAGE RECALL OF INFORMATION			
	3 hours later (%)	3 days later (%)	3 weeks later (%)	3 months later (%)
Telling and showing together	85	65	28	16
Showing (just a letter or picture)	72	10	7	3
Telling (just voice)	70	10	7	3

So couple these statistics to what I was saying about your contacts and their efforts to sell on to the boss. They have no chance of success unless they desperately *want* the deal you're proposing. They have no chance of success unless you arm them with a proper selling Proposal, complete with all relevant sales literature and specification sheets, in a format which will enable the boss to pick it up cold, read it, ask a few questions of your contact and say, 'Yes, we'll buy this.'

What chance of winning have you got if you *don't* - and your competitors *do*?

What to do when there's you, your contact and his Board

From your point of view, you're up against the same set of problems that you faced when your contact had to sell on to the boss. Except this time your contact has a bigger problem. Instead of just one boss, with pet things that turn him or her on and off, we now have several bosses, each with different backgrounds, expertise, attitudes, vested interests and phobias.

Some of them, if it's a highly technical Proposal, won't understand the first thing about the equipment you're proposing, but they'll still expect to make a contribution to the decision-making process - and they'll certainly understand your Financial Justification figures if you've done them correctly.

The very least you need to do when faced with this situation is to make sure that every member of the Board has a copy of your Proposal, in *advance* of the Board Meeting, if a formal meeting has been scheduled during which your Proposal, and your competitors' proposals, are due to be considered. If your competitors haven't taken the trouble to do this, you're going to win hands down.

What to do when there's...

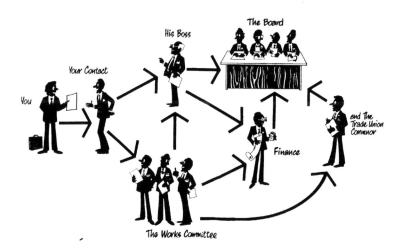

This is an extremely 'popular' situation, meaning it occurs all too frequently! You sell to a single middle-management contact, who then has to sell to the boss. But your contact is also a member of the Works Committee, and your deal is discussed in committee.

The Works Committee can communicate directly with the boss - and does so daily. The boss can communicate directly with the works committee, but avoids this like the plague.

Then the boss has to sell the deal *again,* both to finance on budgetary grounds and to the Board of Directors on principle. It's called an Investment Proposal. Every medium to large business demands it. The multi-nationals and conglomerates are full of it.

Finance share the same feelings as the boss towards the Works Committee. Finance also has a direct line to the Board of Directors, of course.

Finally, the Works Committee discusses *everything* with the trade union convenor (or convenors; one per trade union) who is probably a Member of the Committee anyway. He or she has a secret passage to the Board of Directors but no one is sure to which Member of the Board.

Now you've really got problems. Conflicts of interest. 'Can't afford it' and 'Not in the departmental budget' objections from finance. Environmental considerations, safety considerations, protection of union members' jobs considerations, resistance to changes in procedures and methods of working, as well as cost/benefit considerations.

And if the deal you are proposing has the temerity to reduce labour requirements, you have no chance at all, even with a good selling Proposal.

Why? Because *you're presenting it to the wrong person.*

Assuming you cannot get in front of the Board of Directors, you have two choices - if you have a Proposal and sound financial justification - the boss or finance. Anyone with close links to the Works Committee or the unions is death to the deal. The nearer the very top you can get the better.

What to do when there's ...

Here you are selling direct to the buying committee. But 'the buying committee' is made up of heads of departments and each department has its own self-interests and a deep-set 'competitive spirit' against other departments. I've seen many a good deal deliberately sabotaged by one department 'tribe' because it saw its own interests or kudos in the company pecking order losing out to another department.

Your selling Proposal and its financial justification has to be pretty powerful to get through this lot. With a traditional legal quotation document you might as well give up before you start.

If you can make sure that your proposals cater equally for the interests of each of the departments involved in the buying committee, so that the *status quo* is maintained, you have the best chance of success. Copies of your Proposal to *everyone,* of course.

That's just a glimpse of the can of worms you're opening when you're selling in this modern, sophisticated world. And if you catch a touch of cynicism in those words, you're dead right. Don't kid yourself that I'm exaggerating. I've only given you five examples out of probably five hundred different selling situations you'll come up against. And there you were, not even thinking about how futile is your simple little quotation, looking more like an invoice, with all your terms and conditions on the back, posted to the prospective customers more often than not.

This book is about *How to Sell your Higher Price*, not about how to lose without really trying. A true 90% loss to turn into a gain, or at least a darned good chance of winning - that's what we're talking about in this chapter.

Proposals are in. Quotations are *out*.

How Committees behave - or misbehave!

Of course, there are many buying committees that perform very effectively, just as there are many middle management contacts who communicate thoroughly and honestly to their bosses and to their boards. What I'm saying is - don't take chances on finding a good one. They're the minority, not the majority. I've been there, on both sides!

Let's look into the committee chamber and see what really happens. The bigger the committee, the worse it gets. Hospital or university boards are really something. They're comprised of a mixture of consultant surgeons and physicians, or professors, the administration chiefs and umpteen 'lay' persons, like the Lord High Sheriff, a couple of JPs and the chairman of the region's Womens' Institute. Every committee has a Chairman who is usually elected to the post for his or her impartiality (and that's a laugh!). Every committee has a Secretary, whose job it is to formulate the agenda, take the minutes and organise the coffee and tea.

The agenda is always the same. Cutting out the formalities, minutes of the last meeting, apologies for absence, etc, the big projects and the big money are at the beginning and the small projects with small money are at the end.

Most big projects for these kinds of committees are highly technical. Which means that only two or three members of the committee know anything about the project in detail. These two or three members monopolise the conversation. They also know that they are all-powerful on the big project. The rest of the committee very quickly get bored and begin doodling on their blotters. Five minutes and the 'experts' call for a vote on the big project. £6 million is okayed with only a casual examination and complete faith in the experts. No, it's not for that reason. The real reason is that all the 'lay' members of the committee who wanted to ask questions wouldn't ask them *for fear of looking stupid in the eyes of their fellow members.*

The meeting progresses Projects are discussed in order of descending value and importance. For the first two hours, most of the 'lay' members haven't made a contribution. And they're getting pretty fed up about that. After all, they're on that committee because they *want* to contribute.

So when the agenda approaches its final items, and the Chairman announces - 'Main gates, re-painting of or 'Mattresses for wards E to C, soft or hard' - these very minor items can consume several hours of heated discussion, because every single member of the committee understands fully the subject and most of the members have been waiting in frustration all day for the opportunity to make their contributions.

Five minutes to okay £5 million. Five hours to decide what colour to paint the main gates! That's committees!

How do you structure your proposals, therefore, if you are going to be up against this kind of thing? Cater for the 'lay' people as well as the 'experts' and make sure every member of the committee has a copy of your Proposal in advance of the meeting. A letter to the Secretary, enclosing the appropriate number of copies, which says: 'This project will, we understand, be discussed at your next full committee meeting on Wednesday, 21 November. Please will you make sure each member of your committee receives a copy of our proposals well in advance of this meeting.'

Full marks to the committee Secretary who turns her agenda upside down and deals with the minor items first. But how is she going to get such a change agreed by the committee?

How to make sure you get paid on time

'While we're on the subject of terms and conditions, you'll see that our one and only term is Payment in 30 days promptly. Can I ask you a question on this? It's important to us because if we can't maintain our cash in-flow, it could jeopardize the service we give our customers, and we'd hate that to happen.

Assuming we go ahead with the order, do you see any problems with your accounts department or computer that would make payment difficult within our normal 30 day terms?

Do you need invoices in by a specific "no later than" day of the month for them to be processed that month?'

See how easy it is to talk money to the people to whom you're selling. If you don't, and you have to chase the customers later for payment, they won't care less about seeing that you get paid on time. But if you get an okay from them when you go through the Proposal, you've also got a commitment from them. And when you telephone them to chase payment, rather than their accounts department, they'll move heaven and earth to honour that commitment to you.

How to deal with 'We can't afford it yet'

This selling technique applies to products that can be leased or sold on hire purchase, as well as for cash. If you sell such products, it *always* behoves you to have set up a deal with one particular finance company so that you can sell the finance rather than have to wait for the finance company's representative to close the sale for you. My ego wouldn't like that and I doubt if yours would either!

So let's assume you're armed to sell any of four ways - cash, lease, lease purchase or hire purchase. You go through the Proposal, your customer agrees step by step, but when you get to the automatic close, 'Can we go ahead, then?' he says - 'Not just yet. We can't afford to buy it *yet*.'

And because of all that financial justification you've put together and just gone through with him, you look him in the eye, surprised, and with full confidence and sincerity you say - 'You can't afford NOT to have it. Look at all these costings we've gone through. It will save you at least £450 a week on your loading and unloading work.'

'Yes, I know, but we still can't afford to buy it yet.'

'Why don't you buy it over two or three years? That way, you'll only need to find 10% of the price now, and you'll be saving far more each month than you'll have to pay out. We can only offer this for widget handlers over £2,000, and our group deal with the Bank of Scotland means our interest rates are the best. Here's what your monthly repayments would be (bring out repayments table). Look, you're going to be in profit even in month one. Is there anyone in finance we can get to now, or can you okay a lease or finance deal without checking with them?'

But try this technique *without* the Proposal's financial justification and see what happens.

Index